General Editors: J. R. MULRYNE
and J. C. BULMAN
Associate Editor: Margaret Shewring

Love's Labour's Lost

Already published in the series

Volumes on most other plays in preparation

Of related interest

Shakespeare in Performance

Love's Labour's Lost

MIRIAM GILBERT

Manchester
University Press
Manchester and New York

Distributed exclusively in the USA and Canada by St. Martin's Press

Published by
Manchester University Press
Oxford Road, Manchester M13 9NR
and Room 400, 175 Fifth Avenue,
New York, NY 10010, USA

Distributed exclusively in the USA by
St. Martin's Press, Inc., 175 Fifth Avenue,
New York, NY 10010, USA

British Library Cataloguing-in-Publication Data
A catalogue record for this book is available
from the British Library

Library of Congress Cataloging-in-Publication Data
Gilbert, Miriam
Love's Labour's Lost/Miriam Gilbert
    p. cm. — (Shakespeare in performance)
Includes bibliographical references and index.
ISBN 0-7190-4624-6 (paperback)
1. Shakespeare, William, 1564-1616. Love's Labour's Lost
2. Shakespeare, William, 1564-1616 — Stage history. I. Title.
II. Series.
PR2822.G5   1992
822.3'3—dc20   92-14074
                                                                            CIP
Paperback edition published 1996

ISBN 0 7190 4624 6 *paperback*

Typeset by
Koinonia Limited, Manchester
Printed in Great Britain
by Biddles Limited, Guildford and King's Lynn

CONTENTS

The illustrations appear between chapters iv and v, pp. 76–77.

SERIES EDITORS' PREFACE

The study of Shakespeare's plays as scripts for performance in the theatre has grown in recent years to become a major interest for many university, college and secondary-school students and their teachers. The aim of the present series is to assist this study by describing how certain of Shakespeare's texts have been realised in production.

The series is not concerned to provide theatre histories. Rather, each contributor has selected a small number of productions of a particular play and studied them comparatively. The productions, often from different periods, countries and media, have been chosen because they are significant interpretations in their own right, but also because they represent something of the range and variety of possible interpretations of the play in hand. We hope that students and theatregoers, by reading these accounts of Shakespeare in performance, may enlarge their understanding of the text and begin, too, to appreciate some of the ways in which practical considerations influence the meanings a production incorporates: the stage the actor plays on, the acting company, the player's own physique and abilities, stage-design and theatre-tradition, as well as the political, social and economic conditions of performance and the expectations of a particular audience.

Any study of a Shakespeare text will reveal only a small proportion of the text's potential meaning. We hope that the effect of this series will be to encourage a kind of reading that is receptive to the ever-varying discoveries theatre interpretation provides.

J. R. Mulryne
J. C. Bulman
Margaret Shewring

PREFATORY NOTE

I am grateful to the series editors for inviting me to undertake this study, for their patience, and especially for their helpful comments and advice. Special thanks should go also to the Shakespeare Centre Library, Stratford-upon-Avon, and its staff, particularly Sylvia Morris and Mary White, who have constantly offered me encouragement as well as their skilled professional help; to Jay Halio, for suggesting my name to the series editors; to The University of Iowa for a summer grant which enabled me to do much of the preliminary research; to Roberta K. Cooper for her assistance in locating material relevant to the 1968 Stratford, Connecticut production; to Bob Taylor of the New York Public Library; to Bobbie Mitchell of the BBC Photograph Library; to the staff at the Folger Shakespeare Library; and to Maurice Daniels who made it possible for me to attend final rehearsals of the 1978 RSC production.

My unseen colleagues on this work include not just teachers and critics, but more actors than I can name, since much of my thinking about the play has been shaped by the productions I have been fortunate enough to see, as well as the one I directed in 1982. Let me acknowledge the longstanding help and friendship of Barbara Hodgdon, with whom I once wrote an unpublished 'dialogue' about Barton's 1978 production; from her I have learned to see and to respond more clearly. My hope is that I can make some of what we saw visible again.

Years ago my father participated in amateur theatricals in a small town in Alabama. I helped him learn his lines by cueing him through his roles, and in return I was allowed, though very young, to attend the performance as long as I agreed not to keep on with the cueing. His love for theatre is but one of his gifts to me. This book is dedicated to my mother and to the memory of my father.

Miriam Gilbert

All references, unless otherwise noted, are to the Arden edition of *Love's Labour's Lost*, edited by Richard David (London, 1951), though I have used the spelling 'Dumaine' rather than 'Dumain'. References to other plays of Shakespeare are taken from the *Signet Classic Shakespeare*, edited by Sylvan Barnet.

CHAPTER I

'As it was presented before her Highness': *Love's Labour's Lost* on the Elizabethan stage

> In this play, which all the editors have concurred to censure, and some
> have rejected as unworthy of our poet, it must be confessed that there
> are many passages mean, childish, and vulgar; and some which ought
> not to have been exhibited, as we are told they were, to a maiden queen.
> But there are scattered through the whole many sparks of genius; nor is
> there any play that has more evident marks of the hand of Shakespeare.
> (Johnson, p. 112)

Samuel Johnson's closing comment on *Love's Labour's Lost* for his
1765 edition of *The Plays of William Shakespeare* is intriguing in its
contradictions. After first criticising 'many passages' as being
'mean, childish, and vulgar', Dr Johnson then praises the play's
'many sparks of genius'. But since the play received no professional
productions between Shakespeare's time and the early nineteenth
century, both Dr Johnson and his readers had to find in the text of
the play alone matter both for censure and for praise. In our time,
as the introduction to the New Penguin Shakespeare (1982) makes
clear, '*Love's Labour's Lost* has finally come into its own. After
more than three centuries of neglect, it stands today among those
Shakespeare plays which can be guaranteed to fill houses, thrill
audiences, and – most difficult of all – please actors' (Kerrigan, p.
7). How scholars, directors, actors, and audiences have come to
such an appreciation, and what qualities they have found to appreciate, is the story underlying this study of selected productions of
Love's Labour's Lost. What emerges from looking at the history of
both scholarship and performance is a sense of continual rediscov-
ery. The play seems to disappear and then reappear, with succeed-

ing centuries finding that the features of the play which once seemed strange or forbidding are now precisely the ones we celebrate.

The problems of the play begin with its extremes of content and style. Unlike other early Shakespearean comedies such as *The Comedy of Errors*, *The Taming of the Shrew* or *A Midsummer Night's Dream*, *Love's Labour's Lost* does not have a complicated plot, but is basically an elaboration of one situation. The King of Navarre and three members of his court, Berowne, Dumaine, and Longaville, take an oath to study for three years, and during that time to see no women. The signing of such an oath seems to demand that four young women will immediately arrive on the scene and so they do – and of course the young men fall in love with them. That is the plot of the play.

But the style is much more complicated. The witty young men and the equally witty young women excel in verbal pyrotechnics, loving to exchange quips and puns and put-downs. They frequently pick up words or phrases from each other and send them back, with top-spin, like skilled tennis players. No sooner does the King define 'the end of study' as 'that to know which else we should not know' (I.i.56) than Berowne challenges him, redefining study so that he can successfully evade the prohibition against eating more than once a day or seeing a woman:

> Come on, then; I will swear to study so,
> To know the thing I am forbid to know;
> As thus, – to study where I well may dine,
> When I to feast expressly am forbid;
> Or study where to meet some mistress fine,
> When mistresses from common sense are hid... (I.i. 59-64)

Berowne even loves to redefine his own words, not just the King's. Having suggested that one studies 'to seek the light of truth' (I.i.75), he then launches into a bravura demonstration that 'Light seeking light doth light of light beguile' (I.i.77), claiming that too much reading causes blindness, and that the sight of a fair woman blinds a man's vision but illuminates his soul.

Adding to the sense of verbal extravagance in the play's 'great feast of languages' (V.i.35) are other game-players, or perhaps chefs: Holofernes, the schoolmaster and Sir Nathaniel, the curate, both of whom adore allusions and Latin phrases; Costard, the rustic swain, who (like Bottom and Dogberry) is guilty of malapropisms; finally Armado, the 'fantastical Spaniard', who not only

[2]

writes but embodies elaborate and romantic terms, and his page, young Moth, who sometimes supports but often undercuts his master's verbal gymnastics. None of these figures, together with Jaquenetta, the country wench loved by Armado, and Dull, the local constable, is essential to the slender romantic plot, except perhaps for Costard, who mis-delivers letters given him by Berowne and Armado. But most of these characters are so sensitive to language, and the games one can play with it, that Nathaniel's description of Dull, 'He hath not eat paper, as it were; he hath not drunk ink' (IV.ii.24-5) applies only to Dull and perhaps Jaquenetta. And it is this eating and savouring of words which has, for many readers, made the play seem at once 'brilliant, high-spirited, and verbally masterful' (Van Doren, p. 58) and 'out of fashion' (Granville-Barker, p. 1). Critics recognise its verbal exuberance, but they do not always admire it, perhaps finding the characters so intoxicated with language that they seem merely witty speakers rather than characters worth exploring. Students find the play 'difficult' to read because of the intricate puns, and directors approach the play, blue pencil in hand, ready to cut lines which seem to them obscure and inaccessible; the play's vulnerability to cutting derives also from the repetition of certain passages (most notably Berowne's long speech at the end of IV.iii) which were clearly revised, but not clearly cancelled.

While such an emphasis on stylistic concerns may seem to isolate *Love's Labour's Lost* from the mainstream of Shakespeare's work, much of the play seems familiar when considered in the context of Shakespeare's early plays and of the major comedies. The four young men in this play seem to anticipate the young men in *Romeo and Juliet*, *The Merchant of Venice*, and *Much Ado About Nothing*, both in their clannishness and in their avoidance of women (to a greater or less extent). Berowne, the most intelligent of the four, is similar to Mercutio, although, unlike Mercutio, he can turn his cynical eye on himself. He also anticipates Benedick in *Much Ado About Nothing* who comments so sharply on love-sickness that he sets himself up as Cupid's next victim. The witty sparring between Berowne and Rosaline looks back to Petruchio and Kate, and forward to Beatrice and Benedick; the open-air setting of the King's park is a version of other forests full of lovers, such as the wood outside Athens or the Forest of Arden; the unwittingly comic and accident-prone 'Pageant of the Nine Worthies' reminds us of the 'Pyramus and Thisbe' playlet in *A Midsum-*

mer Night's Dream. Most of these comparisons imply development, as if Shakespeare were trying out possibilities in *Love's Labour's Lost* and then realising their potential more fully in later comedies: thus these comparisons have led, I think, to a persistent undervaluing of this comedy.

Yet in one aspect, *Love's Labour's Lost* is different from all other Shakespearean comedies, and that is in its ending. Even plays which we call comedies only with hesitation, such as *All's Well that Ends Well* and *Measure for Measure*, end with marriage, and most of the comedies involve multiple marriages, often with family reconciliations thrown in for good measure. But at the end of *Love's Labour's Lost*, the young men who promised – so rashly, one might argue – to forswear the world and study must make that promise real. Instead of three years' study, they agree to 'a twelvemonth and a day' before seeing the women again (V.ii.869). Other Shakespearean comedies emphasise the education of young men, but none insists that the growing-up process must take place *before* the woman, or women, will accept a marriage proposal. Even Bassanio, whom many have suspected of fortune-hunting as well as love, gets married mid-way through the play to Portia; only the consummation of the marriage is delayed. Even Bertram, the callow youth and utter snob who marries Helena but refuses to sleep with or acknowledge her, *does* consummate that marriage and is forgiven at the play's end. But *Love's Labour's Lost* shows us couples parting rather than coming together, and the power of that ending is something that performance history has gradually come to value and to emphasise.

The division between the witty style of the comedy and the defiantly untraditional ending finds an echo in the two famous songs, one of Spring and the other of Winter, with which the play concludes. One might argue that the problem of *Love's Labour's Lost* for both audiences and scholars has been the insistence on seeing the play as essentially springlike only to discover at the end that winter has come as well. The sprightliness of the play has perhaps masked that balance from readers, but perceptive critics (Anne Barton, Ralph Berry, William C. Carroll, D. A. Traversi, to name just a few) have argued convincingly that the play does not suddenly change course, but rather forces the audience to realise, as the young men do, that the world contains both daisies and icicles, merry larks and brooding birds. Thus this comedy, which seems in many ways more artificial than Shakespeare's others, more concerned with affectation and stylistic brilliance, becomes finally the most realistic of all, as it acknowledges that the theatre cannot always solve life's complex relationships. In a play filled with performances both impromptu and planned – the reading aloud of other people's letters, Moth's song, Holofernes' epitaph on the death of the deer, the overhearing scene, the masque of the Muscovites, and, of course, the Pageant of the Nine Worthies – Shakespeare acknowledges the theatre's limitations through Berowne's rueful comment, 'That's too long for a play' (V.ii.870). Only within the world of the theatre do relationships blossom so quickly; in the real world, it is not perpetual springtime. Other Shakespearean endings raise similar questions, with Feste's song, 'The rain it raineth every day', as the prime example of an ending which seems to undercut the 'golden time' at the end of *Twelfth Night*. But that song, like Puck's final speech in *A Midsummer Night's Dream* or Rosalind's Epilogue in *As You Like It*, is outside the main action of the play, while in *Love's Labour's Lost*, it is the main action which insists on the separation rather than the union of the young people. Finding the balance between a play of love and wit and an ending which reminds all of us that winter comes too has been the major achievement by critics – and by productions – in the twentieth century.

While we know that modern audiences have come to see *Love's Labour's Lost* as a theatrical piece which subtly balances the claims of both spring and winter, we can only speculate about the experience of the original audience. Unfortunately, we have no firm evidence about where *Love's Labour's Lost* was first performed, nor when it was written. The title page of the First Quarto of *Love's Labour's Lost*, printed in 1598, advertises the play's delights in time-honoured fashion by appealing to the audience's desire to participate in the pleasures of the elite. By announcing that Queen Elizabeth had seen (with the implication that she may have requested) the play for the Christmas celebrations at court, the printer immediately confers status on the play; by stating that the text is 'newly corrected and augmented' he implies that what the reader will buy is not just an 'old' play but something newly refurbished. To the scholar seeking evidence of when the play was first performed and in what state, the title-page offers some help, but nothing really conclusive. Most chronologies of Shakespeare's works put *Love's Labour's Lost* considerably earlier than 1598 (or

1597, depending on which part of the Christmas celebration the play graced), usually settling for a date around 1594-95. Another court performance occurred in 1605, this time before King James and Queen Anne, again at Christmas-time. But the play was by then obviously a revival, something suggested by Burbage as full of 'wit and mirth' (cf. Lamb, p. 51). The Burbage recommendation of this play for performance, as well as the references in the Second Quarto, published in 1631, to the comedy as 'acted at the Blackfriars and the Globe' imply that the play could well have been first performed in a public theatre. Likewise, the evidence of four stanzas in Robert Tofte's 1598 poem *Alba: The Month's Mind of a Melancholy Lover* which describe clearly *Love's Labour's Lost*, suggests that the play was first staged at a public outdoor theatre, such as Burbage's The Theatre (Hibbard, pp. 1-2), rather than at a private performance.

Other suggestions for the original performance include Harbage's argument that the play dates from as early as 1588-89 and was written for one of the acting companies of boys (Harbage, p. 27), an argument which begins by rejecting the notion of the play as originally designed for court performance or at a private 'great house'. Hibbard suggests that perhaps the play was first produced at one of the Inns of Court, such as Gray's Inn, where, for the Christmas Revels of 1594-95, Shakespeare's company presented *The Comedy of Errors* and, several days later, an entertainment including men dressed in Russian habit took place (Hibbard, pp. 46-7). Did Shakespeare pick up the notion that a 'Masque of Muscovites' would work to even greater comic effect in his play – or did the entertainment committee at Gray's Inn borrow the notion of men in Russian attire from Shakespeare?

What can we learn by listing the various venues associated with or suggested for the original performance of *Love's Labour's Lost*? The first point is that we cannot assume any one particular audience for the play. Though the play's emphasis on elaborate language has led a number of critics to assert that the play was meant for a learned audience, such as one might expect at court, Tofte's poem and the claims of the Second Quarto point more obviously to public performances. And, as Ann Jennalie Cook argues in *The Privileged Playgoers of Shakespeare's London*, audiences in the public theatres were likely to be reasonably well-educated people with enough time and money to attend the theatre in the daytime rather than working full-time (p. 224).

The various venues also lead to the conclusion that the play could be performed almost anywhere since the play's *requirements* for performance are relatively simple. Only one scene requires any particular kind of stage set. In IV.iii Berowne must watch from above as his fellow 'students' successively appear, each reading a love-poem, and then going into hiding as the next lovestruck man appears, but even the need to find three hiding places would work easily on a two-level stage without any additional construction or properties. Otherwise, nothing specific in the way of stage decor is indicated. Although the Princess fusses about the fact that the King will not allow her *inside* his gates, nothing in the text suggests that we see those gates. The bare stage of the Elizabethan theatre can easily be the King's park and for most of the play it does not really matter where in the park we are. The production does need to create a sense of separation between the men's space and that of the women, but the two doors of the Elizabethan theatre could easily serve that function. Once the women arrive, and set up 'housekeeping' somewhere in the park, they would probably continue to enter and exit from that same door, just as in twentieth-century productions the women and men tend to 'claim' one side of the stage and to use that side for their entrances and exits. And in the long final scene, the women need to retire offstage briefly to discard their masks and switch back the favours which they have received from the young men.

IV.iii, the overhearing scene, does require that all four men be on stage at the same time and that, at least to the audience, it look faintly plausible that they do not see each other. The stage directions from the Quarto are simple: '*Enter Berowne with a paper*; *The King entreth*; *Enter Longauill with papers*. *The King steps aside*; *Enter Dumaine*.' Berowne's lines imply another stage direction when, after Dumaine's entrance, he comments:

All hid, all hid; an old infant play.
Like a demi-god here sit I in the sky,
And wretched fools' secrets heedfully o'er-eye. (IV.iii.75-7)

Each man hides as the next comes in and Berowne's line indicates that he is *above* the others. John Kerrigan suggests that Berowne could be in the 'lords' room', above and behind the stage (p. 199) while G. R. Hibbard mentions the possibility of a climbable property tree, such as Marston intended for *The Fawn*, his 1605 comedy (p. 165). We know that a portable 'arbour', solid enough to hold the weight (actually the dead weight) of the murdered Horatio is a requirement for Kyd's *The Spanish Tragedy*, probably written in the late 1580s. Moreover, Ben Jonson's early comedy *The Case is Altered* (first printed in quarto, 1609, but presumably dating from 1597-98) includes a scene in which Peter Onion, a servant, hides in a tree from the miserly Jaques and from the threat (kept offstage) of Garlic the mastiff; while Jaques questions Juniper, another servant who had been with Onion, Onion keeps up a punning commentary ('I fear not Garlic; he'll not bite Onion, his kinsman') very similar to Berowne's comments on his three infatuated friends. The 1598 inventory of the properties held by the Lord Admiral's Men mentions 'j baye tree' (*Henslowe's Diary*, p. 319) which allows for the possibility that Berowne hid in an onstage tree, either brought on for the occasion, or perhaps there from the beginning as part of the 'outdoor' setting, though scholars still disagree about whether stage trees are fictive or actual constructions (*Henslowe's Diary*, Reynolds, Habicht, Rhodes). The obvious hiding places for the King and Longaville are, as both Kerrigan and Hibbard note, the two downstage pillars supporting the canopy over the stage. Given the relative simplicity of producing this scene in the Elizabethan theatre, Bernard Shaw's strictures on the scene, growing out of an 1886 amateur production, are particularly amusing:

> The only absolutely impossible situation was that of Biron hiding in the tree to overlook the king, who presently hides to watch Longaville, who in turn spies on Dumain; as the result of which we had three out of the four gentlemen shouting 'asides' through the sylvan stillness, No. 1 being inaudible to 2, 3, and 4; No. 2 audible to No. 1, but not to 3 and 4; No. 3 audible to 1 and 2, but not to No. 4; and No 4 audible to all the rest, but himself temporarily stone deaf. Shakespear has certainly succeeded in making this arrangement intelligible; but the Dramatic Students' stage manager did not succeed in making it credible. For Shakespear's sake one can make-believe a good deal; but here the illusion was too thin. Matters might have been mended had Biron climbed among the foliage of the tree instead of affixing himself to the trunk in an attitude so precarious and extraordinarily prominent that Dumain (or perhaps it was Longaville), though supposed to be unconscious of his presence, could not refrain from staring at him as if fascinated for several seconds. (*Shaw on Shakespeare*, p. 114)

The scene works not because it is credible but because visual conventions come into play for the audience. Just as Oberon tells us, 'I am invisible; / And I will overhear their conference' (*A Midsummer Night's Dream*, II.i. 186-7), so too in IV.iii of *Love's Labour's Lost* we need only to see the character 'stand aside' for him to become hidden as he wishes. Moreover, the characters are so absorbed in their own problems that it looks entirely feasible for them not to see the person or persons already on stage. Only Berowne has enough distance from his own feelings to mock them rather than to wallow in them. His soliloquy at the beginning of IV.iii shows us that he can call himself a 'fool' and a 'sheep' and realise that he is trapped by his own feelings. But although the King speaks of his 'folly' when he drops his paper, Longaville calls himself 'forsworn', and Dumaine says he 'would forget' Katharine, all of them are really more interested in their feelings and their sonnets than in anything else. Such self-absorption is plausible, and we watch the set-up of the scene with delight, knowing that successive 'disappearances' will create successive revelations – as indeed they do.

The last scene of *Love's Labour's Lost* also requires nothing special in the way of a permanent stage setting; and, given the way in which the four couples meet, separate, regroup to watch the Nine Worthies, and separate again, a relatively empty stage seems not merely possible but necessary. The scene with the four lords as Muscovites requires only that the four couples betake themselves to different parts of the stage to create the sense of four private wooings. The Worthies might set up a stage on which to present their pageant, but even a curtain held up by, say, Dull and the Forester would work equally well (as it did in the 1990 RSC production, directed by Terry Hands). The Elizabethan thrust stage almost invites each of the Worthies to come forward: Costard/Pompey offers his armour to the Princess, Moth/Hercules gets so involved in strangling his snake(s) that Holofernes has to get him offstage, and both Holofernes/Judas and Armado/Hector reply so directly to the onstage audience of hecklers, that they seem to be *with* them, rather than separate from them. Only perhaps Sir Nathaniel, already 'o'erparted' with Alexander the Great, might want to stay as close to the 'curtain' or 'onstage' area as possible. Marcade's entrance could easily be made through either of the upstage doors.

But if the play demands little in the way of stage sets and thus lends itself easily to performance in a variety of settings, it does create major work for the costumers. This emphasis on costume, rather than setting, suits a play which emphasises fashions in speech; Berowne famously links the worlds of clothes and language when he renounces 'Taffeta phrases, silken terms precise, / Three-piled hyperboles, spruce affectation, / Figures pedantical' (V.ii.406-8). Taffeta, silk, and the heavy velvet implied by 'three-piled' are all fabrics associated with the upper classes – and may derive from the luxury of the costumes worn by the King's court and the French visitors. Moreover, they are also fabrics familiar to anyone who browses through the lists of costumes in *Henslowe's Diary*, lists which indicate that such fabrics were readily, if expensively, available:

> *Item*, j orenge taney satten dublet, layd thycke with gowld lace.
> *Item*, 1 blew tafetie sewt.
> *Item*, j payr of carnatyon satten Venesyons, layd with gold lace...
> *Item*, Harey the fyftes vellet gowne... .(p. 317)

Even more noticeable are the implications of elaborate costumes for the men when they disguise themselves as Muscovites. We hear first from Boyet that they are 'disguised', a word repeated by the Quarto stage directions, 'Enter Black-moores with musicke, the Boy with a speach, and the rest of the Lordes disguysed.' Katharine asks the seemingly speechless Longaville, 'What! was your visor made without a tongue?' (V.ii.242) and Rosaline asks Berowne, later in the scene, 'Which of the visors was it that you wore?' (V.ii.385), indicating that the men's disguises include face-masks. Similarly, all the women, following the Princess's instruction, 'we will every one be mask'd' (V.ii. 127), wear or hold masks, probably of 'rich taffeta' if we hear Boyet's reply to Moth (V.ii.159) as a description of those masks. Rosaline speaks of the 'Muscovites in shapeless gear' (V.ii.303), implying that the men's disguises were loose and baggy.

Other costumes called for by the text involve the costumes for the Nine Worthies; we hear of Pompey's shield, Alexander's scutcheon (coat of arms, probably on his shield), and Hector's armour. The inventory list for the Lord Admiral's Men in 1598 contains items similar to ones that the Worthies might have used:

> a lion skin (Costard needs a leopard skin and head for Pompey)
> assorted armour
> 1 snake, (probably for a play called *1 Hercules* – although the text does not exist, it seems that the infant Hercules strangled a snake, as Moth will do. See *Henslowe's Diary*, pp. 319-21).

But the existence of stage armour (surely a necessity for any Elizabethan acting company) does not necessarily imply complete or authentic costumes for the Pageant. Unlike the mechanicals in *A Midsummer Night's Dream*, who seem to have thought about the play for longer than an afternoon, Armado, Holofernes, Sir Nathaniel, Costard and Moth clearly have not had much time to whip up costumes or even to memorise their lines. As the text makes clear, Costard has almost managed that feat, but Sir Nathaniel is having major trouble coping with the lines at all. So in production, the Worthies might well appear in their own clothes with pieces of armour over them. Perhaps they brought in yet other pieces of costume or perhaps some decorative props for the final songs, the dialogue between the Owl and the Cuckoo, but nothing in the text specifically insists on more spectacle. Still, if an inventory list can have a dragon for *Doctor Faustus*, a bull's head, and a black dog, perhaps small birds might be easily available (*Henslowe's Diary*, pp. 319-21).

Several other costume details emerge from the text. When the women appear in II.i, Maria must be wearing white, so that Longaville can ask about her (II.i. 196). Rosaline wears a cap, since that is how Berowne identifies her, 'What's her name in the cap?' (II.i. 209), even though his earlier conversation suggests that he knows exactly who she is. Both the Princess (IV.i.1) and Berowne (IV.iii.1) refer to the King out hunting which may suggest that he has changed into a hunting costume. The references to hunting in IV.i might also imply a costume change for the Princess and her ladies, with all appearing in something appropriate for that sport – or they could just carry bows and arrows. It is traditional in contemporary productions for Marcade to be all in black; *Henslowe's Diary* makes clear that elaborate black costumes were available, even for a single scene (p. 223), so it seems probable that Marcade's was such a one. The Princess is quick to understand his errand and even finishes the sentence for him:

Marcade: The king your father –
Princess: Dead, for my life!
Marcade: Even so: my tale is told. (V.ii.711-13)

His black costume announces the King's death even before his grave tone and quiet words do so. Marcade's entrance late in the play may also take advantage of the fading light of an afternoon performance at an outdoor playhouse. When Berowne remarks after Marcade's line, 'The scene begins to cloud' (V.ii.714), his words are metaphorical in terms of the stage action but may have been literally true for the outdoor audience.

We can infer, then, that the first production – or productions – of *Love's Labour's Lost* followed conventions of staging that we

[11]

associate with the Elizabethan stage. The play appealed visually through gorgeous costumes rather than through elaborate settings, and through the quick movement from one group of characters to another. Indeed, the beginning of IV.i, when the Princess enters for the hunt with the question 'Was that the king, that spurr'd his horse so hard / Against the steep-up rising of the hill?' (1-2), suggests that she enters just in time to see someone leave the stage; it is not the King, but probably Berowne, exiting from the previous scene. At the end of IV.i Costard hears a 'shout within' (actually printed as 'shoot within'), cries 'Sola, sola', and rushes off, presumably to watch the hunting/shooting, and immediately Holofernes, Sir Nathaniel and Dull come in from watching the shooting, and commenting on it. And at the end of their scene, Holofernes comments 'the gentles are at their game, and we will to our recreation'(IV.ii.158-9), inviting us to believe that we will see more hunting. Then Berowne enters with the words, 'The king he is hunting the deer; I am coursing myself' (IV.iii.1-2) and we are into the hunt for the heart, rather than the hart.

But the play's real life on stage for the Elizabethan audience was a verbal rather than a visual one. The Princess's description of the slightly barbed interchange between Rosaline and Katharine (V.ii.19-28) as 'a set of wit well-played' (V.ii.29) could well apply to many moments when the play's abundant energy comes from speakers who delight in witty thrusts and counter-thrusts. I have already mentioned Berowne's opening challenges both to the King's proclamation and the King's language. So infectious is his wit that soon the other men join in, picking up his rhythms, his verbal oppositions, and his rhymes:

King: How well he's read to reason against reading!
Dumaine: Proceeded well to stop all good proceeding!
Longaville: He weeds the corn, and still lets grow the weeding. (I.i. 94-6)

The effect of such language games is, from the first, to make the audience listen carefully. By the time Dull enters with Armado's letter, we have become accustomed to the balanced wit of the young men and so are ready to enjoy both the puns of Costard and the elaboration of the obvious in Armado's letter. While the *point* of the letter is to accuse Costard of misconduct, both the writer and the readers seem more interested in style, or, as Berowne puts it, 'How low soever the matter, I hope in God for high words' (I.i. 190-1). 'High words' are exactly what Armado adores, whether he's addressing the King as 'Great deputy, the welkin's vicegerent, and sole dominator of Navarre, my soul's earth's God, and body's fostering patron' (I.ii. 216-18), characterising his mood, 'besieged with sable-coloured melancholy' (I.ii. 227), or specifying the time of the incident as 'about the sixth hour; when beasts most graze, birds best peck, and men sit down to that nourishment which is called supper' (I.ii. 231-3). Armado's 'high words' when writing to the king continue in his polysyllabic conversation with his young servant Moth: 'I spoke it, tender juvenal, as a congruent epitheton appertaining to thy young days, which we may nominate tender' (I.ii. 13-15). Only when he confronts the country wench, Jaquenetta, with whom he has fallen in love, does he shrink into monosyllabic wooing – and the sharp contrast is extremely funny.

The fascination with *how* people express themselves, perhaps even more than *what* they say, is obvious throughout the play. We sense the immediate connection (whether of attraction or competition) between Berowne and Rosaline in their echoing phrases of II.i; we hear the pretentiousness of Holofernes in the Latin phrases slipped easily into sentence after sentence – and his condescension in the translations he supplies; further, we savour the sonnets of the young men, noting that Dumaine cannot even manage such an intricate form and settles for tetrameter couplets, while the King's passion makes him exceed the normal fourteen lines and go on for an extra couplet. Because the characters and their costumes, not the setting, provide all the visual interest, we focus on them – and because they enjoy language so much and comment so frequently on the language of others, we listen closely.

Such emphasis on language is one of the distinguishing features of Shakespeare's contemporary, John Lyly (1554-1606), whose well-known prose work, *Euphues* (1578), embodied a highly symmetrical style, so distinctive that it came to be called 'euphuistic', and so noticeable that Falstaff could easily parody it in *Henry IV, Part 1*. In his plays, as Peter Saccio has noted, Lyly often creates not just parallel dialogue but parallel actions; in *Gallathea* (1588), 'three of the nymphs enter serially to soliloquize on their love-stricken state and then discover their common condition', while in *Love's Metamorphosis* (*c*. 1590) 'three couples enter serially, each man passionately pleading his suit and each nymph contemptuously rejecting him' (Saccio, p. 134). Saccio connects these actions to the climactic scene in *Love's Labour's Lost* where the hidden Berowne overhears first the King, then Longaville, and then Dumaine each read a sonnet confessing his love, as well as to the swearing of oaths of love by Orlando, Phebe, and Silvius in V.ii of *As You Like It* (p. 134); in Shakespeare, even more than in Lyly, the ostentatious parallelism creates laughter.

As Jocelyn Powell suggests in an illuminating article on Lyly, the notion of style as action is grounded in the Elizabethan love of play and display, of showing off one's expertise in dancing, music, chess, cards, or conversation. Castiglione's *The Book of the Courtier* (1528, trans. 1561) emphasises the need to be a good conversationalist, while Stephano Guazzo's *Civil Conversation*, translated into English in 1581, noted the importance of witty speaking, through the use of variety and decorative phrases. The Elizabethan habit of keeping a commonplace book in which one could note down aphorisms and phrases that would turn up later in conversation suggests how prevalent was the interest in sounding witty. Sir Andrew Aguecheek in *Twelfth Night*, hopelessly hanging around Olivia's house in hopes of wooing her, is alert to notice the speech of the disguised Viola and to comment on particular words: 'Odors', 'pregnant,' and 'vouchsafed' – I'll get 'em all three all ready' (III.i.88-9). A similar appreciation of fine language turns up when Holofernes congratulates Armado on his elegant variation for the common word 'afternoon': 'The posterior of the day, most generous sir, is liable, congruent, and measurable for the afternoon: the word is well culled, chose; sweet and apt, I do assure you, sir; I do assure' (V.i. 83-6).

Thus, for Shakespeare's audiences, both in the public theatres and at court, *Love's Labour's Lost* must have seemed, in the words of the First Quarto's title-page, 'a pleasant conceited comedie', especially when we remember that 'conceit' implied fanciful and imaginative metaphors. They saw elegantly dressed courtiers exchanging witty remarks; they picked up the Latin tags of Holofernes; they enjoyed the 'mistakes', unconscious and conscious, of Costard; they savoured the verbal one-upmanship of Moth. With Armado, they might well have said: 'Now, by the salt wave of the Mediterraneum, a sweet touch, a quick venue of wit! Snip, snap, quick and home! It rejoiceth my intellect. True wit!' (V.i. 54-6). An audience used to listening rather than reading as its primary way of receiving ideas would enjoy *Love's Labour's Lost* in the same way that people who play tennis, even as amateurs, appreciate the subtleties of a well-played Wimbledon match. There is something exciting about watching professionals at work: the stichomythic banter between Berowne and Rosaline in II.i sets them up as contenders equally skilled at come-ons and put-downs; the elaboration of epithets for Cupid from Berowne (III.i) reveals simultaneously that he is in love and that he is angry at finding himself in love; Boyet's description of the offstage rehearsal of the Muscovites (V.ii) shows him to be a shrewd observer and, even better, a marvellous raconteur.

In addition to such displays of aristocratic verbal wit, the play offers the audience other forms of wit. We remember that Dr Johnson complained of passages 'which ought not to have been exhibited, as we are told they were, to a maiden queen' (p. 112), and certainly the play's sexual punning is constant and obvious, so much so that at one point Maria complains to Costard and Boyet, 'Come, come, you talk greasily; your lips grow foul' (IV.i.138). Boyet is the master of sexual innuendo, whether trying to convince the Princess that the King has fallen in love with her, or flirting with the ladies, or teasing Rosaline; but Rosaline and Katharine trade accusations of unchastity (V.ii.24-5), and Berowne's defence of Rosaline's beauty sends Dumaine into a schoolboy's 'dirty joke':

> Berowne: O! if the street were paved with thine eyes,
> Her feet were much too dainty for such tread.
> Dumaine: O vile! then, as she goes, what upward lies
> The street should see as she walk'd overhead. (IV.iii. 274-7)

These lines, and many other references (although, to my mind, fewer than Herbert A. Ellis argues for in *Shakespeare's Lusty Punning in 'Love's Labour's Lost'*), all contain deliberate sexual references. There are also what might be called the unconscious references, at least so far as the characters are concerned, such as Nathaniel's praise of Holofernes' teaching and Holofernes' placid acceptance:

> Nathaniel: Sir, I praise the Lord for you, and so may my parishioners; for their sons are well tutored by you,and their daughters profit very greatly under you; you are a good member of the commonwealth.
> Holofernes: *Mehercle*! if their sons be ingenious, they shall wantno instruction; if their daughters be capable, I will put it to them. (IV.ii. 71-7)

It's difficult to believe that the curate Nathaniel would even imply, let alone think, that Holofernes has any sexual involvement with the daughters 'under' him, although the next phrase certainly allows the audience such a connection, as does Holofernes' 'I will put it to them.'

[15]

Most of all, with Costard, played originally by the best-known comedian of the age, Will Kemp (Wiles, pp. 105-6), the play reminds the audience constantly that 'Such is the simplicity of man to hearken after the flesh' (I.i.214-15), a simplicity which is natural and, as the courtiers learn, undeniable. No sooner have the young men signed the unnatural oath, forbidding themselves the sight of women and forbidding women to enter their sight, than Dull drags on Costard, arrested because he 'sorted and consorted' (as Armado's letter puts it, I.i. 252) with a woman. We cannot be sure whether the 'consorting' involved just speaking to Jaquenetta, or something more intimate. Costard implies the latter, denying her virginity (albeit in the context of trying to wriggle out of the accusation by quibbling over various words for 'woman') and then capping the King's warning, 'This maid will not serve your turn, sir' with 'This maid will serve my turn, sir' (I.i. 289-90), implying that he knows her to be sexually forthcoming. In addition to Costard's sexual puns, he is also remarkable (as are Bottom and Dogberry, two other roles that Kemp played) for his malapropisms: 'therefore welcome the sour cup of prosperity' (I.i. 304); 'if ever I do see the merry days of desolation that I have seen' (I.ii.149-50); and so on. But if he twists and sometimes mutilates language, he can also expose its pretentiousness, as in his memorable comparison of Armado's 'remuneration' to Berowne's 'gardon' where he rightly concludes that the latter tip is 'a 'leven-pence farthing better' (II.i. 165), or in his crushing rejoinder to the 'head lady', the Princess, that she must be the 'chief woman' since she is also 'the thickest' (IV.i. 51). Though Costard confuses Armado's letter and Berowne's, thus setting up the exposure of Berowne as a lover, he nonetheless rises above the situation to escape any blame, 'Walk aside the true folk, and let the traitors stay' (IV.iii. 209). He is, whether unwittingly as with the letters, or wittingly as in the revelation of Jaquenetta's pregnancy (V.ii.667-9), the exposer of others throughout the play, inviting the audience not only to laugh at him, but to laugh with him at those who pretend to knowledge.

In addition to the play's attractiveness as a spirited linguistic game, it also created for Elizabethan audiences, through the French setting, and the names of contemporary historical figures, a tantalising set of topical references. There really was a King of Navarre, though he was named Henri and not Ferdinand. Yet since the name 'Ferdinand' appears only in stage directions and never in the text, it's quite possible that audiences immediately thought of

Henri of Navarre, later Henri IV of France (1553-1610). The Duc de Longueville was an ally of Henry's during the Protestant/Catholic religious wars in France extending through the last half of the sixteenth century, as were two members of the Biron (Berowne) family. Dumaine seems to refer to the Duc de Mayenne, a well-known opponent of Henri IV's, and a character seen on the Elizabethan stage in Marlowe's *The Massacre at Paris* (1593). Though Henri of Navarre did possess a country estate, Nérac, where he was visited in 1578 by his wife, his mother-in-law, and other women, including both a former mistress and a future mistress (cf. Hibbard, p. 50), it is difficult to see how such a visit fits with the announced desire of Shakespeare's King of Navarre to live in celibate study. Indeed, the more details one gathers about the real historical figures, such as the fact that Henri was first a Protestant and then a Catholic, while Du Mayenne was always a fervent Catholic, the less easy it becomes to reconstruct the exact significance that these figures had for Shakespeare's audience.

Scholars have proposed various readings, of which two strike me as persuasive. Henri's switch from Protestantism to Catholicism (in 1593) might well have been seen as oath-breaking of a particularly serious kind, especially to an English audience which had lived through its own period of repression under the Catholic Mary I. The gravity of the oath-breaking by the real Henri might, as Mary Ellen Lamb suggests, thus extend to the breaking of oaths by Shakespeare's Navarre, fictional character though he is. But it is also possible to see what Albert Tricomi calls 'a deliberate contra-topicality, a deliberate inversion of the topical wherein these persons are charmingly transmuted from the French civil war into the fairy-tale world of Nérac' (p. 29). With this reading, the audience smiles at Shakespeare's characters, knowing well how unlike the historical Henri the fictional Ferdinand really is, especially in matters of sexual fidelity and abstinence.

Given the allusions, however the audiences read them, to actual historical figures for some of the play's aristocratic characters, it is therefore not surprising that scholars have tried for years to find connections between the more obviously comic characters and contemporary figures. Richard David's introduction to the Arden edition offers a useful summary of the suggestions developed over many years that Holofernes represents the translator John Florio or perhaps the Cambridge don, Gabriel Harvey, that Moth is the playwright Thomas Nashe, and that the play itself was, in David's words, 'a battle in a private war between court factions' (p. xliii). The problems with such allusions are many, including their assumption that the play was performed primarily at court (thus ignoring the evidence of the Second Quarto's title-page) and the difficulty of proving any of the often strained connections; as Mary Ellen Lamb points out, 'who could prove that Holofernes was *not* Gabriel Harvey?' (p. 53). But the very efforts to find contemporary figures behind the characters of this play, whether soldiers, politicians, playwrights, or teachers, reflects a particular kind of anxiety, the feeling that the play would become more comprehensible if *some* sources could be found, if not for plot, then at least for characters. It's interesting to note that *A Midsummer Night's Dream*, with which *Love's Labour's Lost* shares many qualities, including the lack of a particular literary source, seems not to arouse the same kinds of questions, perhaps because the characters of Theseus and Hippolyta, as well as Oberon, Titania and Puck, have a pre-Shakespearean literary life.

What we cannot know is exactly how Shakespeare intended his original audience to respond to these references, or even whether he expected the audiences, either at the Globe or the Blackfriars, to whisper to themselves, 'Ah, what a wonderful parody of John Florio!' or 'Look at what he's doing with the King of Navarre!' The play has its own internal consistency, and so it is entirely possible to see the irony of the oath-breaking without having ever heard of Henri IV, and to recognise that there is something overblown and pompous about Holofernes without trying to figure out who he *really* is. Since we cannot be sure about the original audience, we cannot therefore assume that the play is an extended 'in-joke', whether academic or political.

Questions about how the audience experienced the play extend also to the play's central love relationships. Tofte's poem, our chief contemporary evidence, reports that 'To everyone (save me) 'twas comical' (quoted by Hibbard, p. 1). Perhaps Tofte is offering an objective description of the audience's reaction, or perhaps he wishes to emphasise his own reaction, 'Whilst tragic-like to me it did befall', as a way of persuading his lady-love to pity him. His poem suggests that the actors portrayed the lovers, 'those entrapped in Cupid's snare' with 'feigned' ease, and complains 'They seemed to grieve, but yet they felt no care', implying that the loss of the lovers at the end seemed merely a surface one. But since Tofte wants to contrast the actors' 'feigning' with his own 'mere truth', his account lacks the objectivity one would want. Still the question he raises and others it implies persist to the present day. Does the play show us men and women who think they are in love with each other, but who are really more in love with their own witty ideas about love? If so, should the loss of such 'love' be seen as appropriate rather than regrettable? Do the two songs at the end, with their evocations of familiar scenes and sounds (and familiar jokes about the cuckold too) manage to reconcile the spectators to an unfamiliarly open-ended play? How seriously does the play ask us to take the opening oaths and the breaking of those oaths? Is the prevailing tone satiric, lighthearted or witty?

The more one asks such questions, the more one becomes aware of the play's complexity, a complexity enacted in the last lines of the play as well as in the concluding action and the songs. The final speech of the play, 'The words of Mercury are harsh after the songs of Apollo' (V.ii.922) points in contrary directions. The god Mercury is associated with conducting the dead to the underworld, and the messenger who announces the death of the French king is named Marcade, probably pronounced Marcadé (cf. Hibbard, p. 48) while Apollo, in Berowne's great fourth-act speech, is the god of love and poetry. So too the very last words, printed only in the Folio, 'You that way; we this way', perhaps a stage direction for the characters separating the men and women, perhaps a comment from stage to playhouse audience reminding them that they now return from the artificial to the real world, suggest contrarieties. The awareness of such contrarieties marks the major academic critical discussions of *Love's Labour's Lost*, beginning with the essay of Anne Barton (then Bobbyann Roesen) on the play in 1953. The essay begins arrestingly and paradoxically:

> In a sense the play has ended; an epilogue has been spoken by Berowne and that haunting and beautiful kingdom created by the marriage of reality with illusion, destroyed, seemingly beyond recall. In the person of Marcade, the world outside the circuit of the park has at last broken through the gates, involving the people of the play in its sorrows and grim actualities, the plague-houses and desolate retreats, the mourning cities and courts of that vaster country overshadowing the tents and the fantastic towers of Navarre. (p. 411)

At first one may wonder what play she could be talking about, but as her essay makes clear, 'plague' and 'desolation' are the play's own words. Moreover, after beginning at the end, she then moves quickly and convincingly to the play's opening lines, reminding us of their preoccupation with Fame, Time, and Death, 'a shadow [that] darkens for a moment the delicate dream landscape of the park'.

A series of books and essays followed Anne Barton's lead in taking *Love's Labour's Lost* seriously. C. L. Barber's *Shakespeare's Festive Comedy* in 1959, Ralph Berry's 'The Words of Mercury' in 1969, William C. Carroll's *The Great Feast of Language in 'Love's Labour's Lost'* in 1976, all focus attention on the language of the play, but see it in terms of what that language reveals about the characters and how the use of language is itself a major theme of the play. Such concentration on the meaning of the play itself, rather than on discovering its topical background (a practice that began in 1747 when Warburton proposed the Holofernes/Florio connection) or on placing the play in the context of other Shakespearean comedies and thus, almost inevitably, relegating it to the sidelines or treating it as an anomaly because of its ending, has accompanied and perhaps stimulated the many revealing productions of the play in the twentieth century. Indeed, the disappearance of the play from the stage in the late seventeenth and the entire eighteenth century might be compared to its disappearance from sustained critical commentary – each reflecting the other. And it is worth noting that the revival of interest in the play on stage in the twentieth century in fact preceded Anne Barton's influential essay. Modern directors seem particularly sensitive to the play's contradictions and switches of mood, as the later discussion of productions by Peter Brook and John Barton will suggest. But the Elizabethan and Jacobean audiences would equally have relished those oppositions, and one of the mysteries of theatre history is why it took 200 years before audiences could again enjoy *Love's Labour's Lost* in the theatre.

CHAPTER II

Disappearance and reappearance: *The Students* and Sadler's Wells, 1857

Between the first decade of the seventeenth century and the third decade of the nineteenth century, *Love's Labour's Lost* seems to have disappeared from the English stage. It is, conspicuously, the *only* play of Shakespeare's not performed between 1700 and 1800 (Hogan, p. 716); such a distinction raises the question, 'What was it about *Love's Labour's Lost* which so discouraged or repelled actors and directors for 200 years?' If we can understand cuts in the texts used for modern productions as clues to the director's interpretation, we can equally use the complete ignoring of a play as the signal for interpretation. Why should *this* play be seen as unworthy of the stage, especially when our own century has found it so playable? Admittedly, not everyone in the eighteenth century overlooked *Love's Labour's Lost*. In 1771 the eminent actor David Garrick commissioned a musical version, which cut about 800 lines of the text, omitted the Nine Worthies, and created solos for most of the characters, but that version was never staged (Stone). About ten years earlier, in 1762, an anonymous adaptation of the play, *The Students*, was published, but though the title-page describes the play as a 'Comedy, Altered from Shakespeare's *Love's Labours Lost* and Adapted to the Stage', there is no evidence at all that this version was ever performed. Yet a quick look at *The Students* is instructive, primarily to see what parts of the play remained, and what parts did not. With these cuts in mind, it may be possible to come to some understanding of why *Love's Labour's Lost* should have disappeared from the stage for so long.

While *The Students* follows the basic structure of *Love's Labour's Lost* with the four young men's plans for study interrupted by the arrival of the four young women, it differs significantly from Shakespeare's play in several ways. It is considerably shorter, with approximately 1,625 lines compared to Shakespeare's 2,785. Though most of the lines *are* from Shakespeare, there are some new ones added, and some rearrangement of scenes. Most of Armado's punning with Moth goes. Holofernes and Sir Nathaniel disappear completely, with some of Holofernes' lines spoken by the Player (a new minor role), who confers with Armado about the pastime to be presented to the Princess. Dull puts in a brief appearance and gets a memorable line when, in answer to Armado's question about his profession, he replies, 'I am by trade a constable, and by profession a rat-catcher' (IV.i). A new character, Timothy Clod, appears, though he is not named in the Dramatis Personae; his sole purpose seems to involve taking a coat to Costard. Biron (Berowne) buys that coat from him and spends a number of scenes disguised as Costard. Such a disguise allows for several episodes of mistaken identity, including one in which Biron-as-Costard tries to convince the real Costard that he is not Costard, but someone else; Biron even offers to find him another name. Later in the same scene, Dumaine meets Costard, asks about the letter that Dumaine sent to Catherine (which has, of course, been taken by the disguised Biron), and beats up the real Costard until he admits to having taken the letter. Such a replay of the mistakes in *The Comedy of Errors*, a play as full of plot as *Love's Labour's Lost* is lacking in one, suggests that the adaptor saw the disguise of Biron as a chance to put in some entertaining comic scenes. And though *The Comedy of Errors* was never one of the big theatrical successes of the eighteenth century, it was performed at least fifty-two times, sometimes in a version known as *The Twins* (Hogan, p. 718).

While adding the new complications, however, the adaptor reduced Shakespeare's play by omitting the masque of the Muscovites, the Pageant of the Worthies, and the entrance of Marcade; even more surprisingly, the surefire scene of the play, IV.iii, the overhearing scene, is gone. In its place, Biron, disguised as Costard, gives the sonnets of the King, Dumaine, and Longaville to the women, hears them read aloud, and also hears the women confess their love for the young men. But the Princess then points out that they should return the sonnet/letters, since ''Tis wisdom to conceal, where knowledge wou'd/Betray our weakness' (III.ii). Biron/ Costard thus receives the men's letters again; and in IV.ii he comes in, still as Costard, and hands the letters back, making sure, however, to give the letters to the wrong men so that each realises that the others have broken their vows. Thus the adaptor uses the Biron/ Costard disguise to expose the King, Dumaine, and Longaville, but keeps Biron's power supreme because his love is never exposed in the same way.

Biron's overhearing of the women's confessions is but one instance of the rewriting of the complex balance of power which Shakespeare's play presents. *Love's Labour's Lost* makes clear that Rosaline, Maria and Katharine have heard about Berowne, Longaville and Dumaine and are presumably interested in them, but *The Students*, after using the relevant speeches (II.i.40-76), then adds new ones in which the women mock the men's studies. Moreover, Catherine suggests, 'Suppose, we practise all our little arts, / To raise them from this legarthy [*sic*]' (I.iii), and Rosaline adds that they should flirt with the men and then disappoint them. Later, in III.ii (a revision of Shakespeare's hunting scene, IV.i), Rosaline exults in her power over Biron: 'Biron is my slave, / He has no will, but I have power to guide; / He has no joy, but when I deign to smile, / He has no oath, but what he swears to me.' Her pride receives an immediate come-uppance when the disguised Biron enters with letters for the Princess, Maria and Catherine, but none for Rosaline – and the other women throw her boastful phrases back at her.

By rewriting the scenes with the women to suggest first that they *plan* to flirt with the men, then that they are pleased to receive the sonnet/letters (or, in Rosaline's case, disappointed not to get one), and finally that they are in love but will pretend not to be, the adaptor eliminates the moral, intellectual, and emotional superiority that Shakespeare's women so strikingly possess. Shakespeare's women do not set out to capture the men, and when they receive presents and poems, they wittily comment on them, suggesting an emotional detachment from the situation. Their disguises for the Muscovite scene represent, as Shakespeare's Princess puts it, 'mock for mock' (V.ii. 140). And when the women finally receive what sound like sincere proposals from the men, they insist that such sincerity be tested by time – the year of trial. But the final scene in *The Students* rewrites the events of Shakespeare's play even further to set up a happy ending. Biron steps forward to reveal that he heard the women confess their love: 'as Costard I o'erheard them'. Rosaline still holds out, insisting that he will have to wait for her, 'A man, my lord, who cannot love a year, / Is ne'er entitled to a woman's love', only to meet with Biron's threat to leave her entirely. So she pleads with him to stay, trapped into the capitulation by Biron's knowledge of the earlier scene and by her own desires: 'Perhaps – I was but joking.' The closing lines go to Biron and offer a tidy conclusion in place of Shakespeare's open ending:

> Our wooing now doth end like an old play;
> Jack hath his Jill; these ladies' courtesie
> Hath nobly made our sport a Comedy.

Other textual rearrangements add to the power of the men rather than of the women, particularly the use made of Berowne's long speech from IV.iii of Shakespeare's play, the speech which ends up arguing that women's eyes 'are the books, the arts, the academes, / That show, contain, and nourish all the world' (348-9). Since the adaptor has cut the overhearing scene, but obviously wishes to retain the words, he must find other places for that speech and he puts the lines about women's eyes into I.i when Berowne is still objecting to withdrawing from the world. But the bulk of the speech appears in the final scene – and its re-placement changes its meaning almost completely. The adaptor begins the final scene with Shakespeare's V.ii. 771 ('We have received your letters full of love'), the men's proposals, and the women's demands for penance. As in Shakespeare's play, Rosaline tells Biron he must make jokes in a hospital. Instead of replying directly, he says (in what sounds like an awkward transition), 'I first must make a speech to these grave signiors', and he launches into 'Have at you then, affection's men-at-arms!' The more Biron praises women's beauty, the more his speech sounds like an attempt to persuade the women to change their minds rather than a rationalisation of the men's broken vows.

In short, by moving the proposals and penances to the beginning of the scene, by eliminating Marcade altogether, and by changing the balance of power between men and women, the adaptor rewrites the final scene of *Love's Labour's Lost* to create not just a happy ending, but one which emphasises traditional views of male/female relationships, particularly the idea of wooing as a war that men will win. In Shakespeare's play, Berowne calls his companions 'affection's men-at-arms' and later urges, 'Advance

your standards, and upon them, lords! / Pell-mell, down with them!'
(IV.iii. 286, 363-4) while the King echoes him with 'Saint Cupid,
then! and, soldiers, to the field!' (IV.iii. 362). In *The Students*,
Rosaline calls herself 'an easy conquest, as a man cou'd wish for'
and Biron drives home the moral with clarity: 'My liege, you see
how / Woman yields, when woo'd in proper terms.' The Princess's
capitulation echoes Rosaline's, 'We shall not disobey, what you
command.' Both women sound strikingly like the tamed Kate in
The Taming of the Shrew, just as Biron's lines remind us of
Petruchio's 'awful rule, and right supremacy' (V.ii.108) as well as
his earlier comment, ''Tis a world to see / How tame, when men and
women are alone, / A meacock wretch can make the curstest shrew'
(II.i.304-6). Shakespeare's women remain both untamed and
unattained; but only the Epilogue to *The Students*, spoken by
Rosaline (perhaps a borrowing from *As You Like It* where Rosalind
has the final word), reminds us that the women have, on one level,
succeeded:

> Well, 'tis agreed – deny it, if you can –
> We spoil the scholar – but we make the man.

While a number of the cuts made in Shakespeare's play focus on
the very qualities of the play which make it atypical among Shakespeare's comedies – the grim presence of death as presented (perhaps even represented) by Marcade and the anti-comic resolution
with couples parting instead of wedding – it is worth noting that
The Students also eliminates moments that might seem particularly
funny, such as the masque of the Muscovites and the Pageant of the
Nine Worthies. Why should the adaptor cut these? Having already
revised the women into more traditional and submissive roles, the
adaptor may have noticed that the masque of the Muscovites shows
the young men as immature, and the Pageant reveals their capacity
for mean, even nasty, behaviour. In Shakespeare's play, the silliness and bullying demonstrated by the men almost demand that
they grow up – and grow up before their proposals of marriage are
accepted. While the men in *The Students* are certainly immature
(with both the King and Dumaine looking for relaxation from study
even before they have signed the oath), they lack the bullying lines
of their Shakespearean counterparts and so the final marriages
seem more credible. Shakespeare's overhearing scene pokes fun at
all of the men, including Berowne, but the author of *The Students*
seems to want to avoid such ridicule of his male characters. He

[25]

keeps Berowne particularly safe from ridicule by giving him not just the vantage point of a 'demigod in the sky' but the advantage of disguise as well. Thus, in *The Students*, Biron can trick Costard, spy on the women, *and* trap the women in their broken oaths, while in *Love's Labour's Lost*, Berowne's momentary triumph over his fellow courtiers quickly disappears when his own letter is brought in by Costard and Jaquenetta and, in tearing it up, he reveals his own love-guilt.

Though we can never know precisely why *Love's Labour's Lost*, or even a revision of it, failed to intrigue theatre managers, actors, and audiences for so long, some speculations may be in order. One possibility is the problem of authorship, since influential editors of Shakespeare (notably Alexander Pope) questioned whether or not Shakespeare had written all of *Love's Labour's Lost*. Moreover, the lack of a spectacular leading role for either male or female actors – a lack which, in the twentieth century, has often led to productions praised for ensemble effort – may have contributed to the overlooking of the play. Even a play such as *Pericles*, which did not appear in the First Folio, was frequently performed in the last half of the seventeenth century because it provided a wonderful opportunity for Thomas Betterton to display his acting range (Taylor, pp. 21-3). Though Dr Johnson could implicitly reject Pope's judgement of the authorship problem by claiming 'nor is there any play that has more evident marks of the hands of Shakespeare', he objected to many passages which he found 'mean, childish, and vulgar' (Johnson, p. 112). Since Dr Johnson's hostility to puns is well known, and this play is full of them, the passages to which he so objects are probably the extended series of puns, which turn up in scene after scene (Hibbard, pp. 2-3). Certainly it is noticeable that the adaptor of *The Students* eliminated as many such passages as he could.

The failure to end with the four marriages which seem promised and inevitable may also have made the play less appealing to eighteenth-century tastes. This was, after all, the century which created Nahum Tate's *King Lear*, with its romance between Cordelia and Edgar, as well as Garrick's version of *Romeo and Juliet* in which, as in Otway's and Cibber's versions, Juliet woke up before Romeo's death and the two lovers had yet another scene together before they both died (Levenson, pp. 17-30). In a century which made famous tragedies either non-tragic or more pathetic, *Love's Labour's Lost*'s ending with the entrance of Marcade, the announcement of France's death, and the subsequent parting of the lovers must have seemed much too far away from comic conventions to be acceptable. Indeed, it is *Love's Labour's Lost*'s flouting of conventions both of society and of theatre that the adaptor of *The Students* successfully removes. Men and women retain their traditional roles, and a comedy ends with multiple marriages.

Whatever the reasons for its neglect, *Love's Labour's Lost* did not return to the London stage until 1839 when Madame Vestris, the singer, actress, and theatre manager, presented it as her opening production at Covent Garden, a venue previously managed by the eminent tragedian, William Charles Macready. It was also her first production ever of a Shakespeare play, as her previous management of the much smaller Olympic Theatre had concentrated on often elaborate productions of light entertainment. Clifford John Williams speculates on the motivation which may have led Madame Vestris and her husband, the actor Charles John Mathews, to undertake *Love's Labour's Lost*:

> Somewhat overplaying their hand in trying to prove that they were fitting custodians of the National Drama, the Mathewses chose *Love's Labour's Lost*. The choice of Shakespeare is understandable if not inevitable. The choice of play is rather insanely commendable, and anyone can see the arguments that led to it: a play not performed since Shakespeare's own time; a play not calling for a leading actor that they had not got; a play depending on the team work that they had always fostered and worked for, and a play giving Planché a fine opportunity for some costume lessons. (p. 155)

Since Madame Vestris unfortunately chose to close the top gallery (where the price was one shilling) at the same time as she opened the new season, she faced an extraordinarily hostile audience on 30 September 1839. The combination of the unfamiliar play and the shouting audience did not produce success, and even though the shilling gallery was re-opened, the production ran only eight more times.

Still, Madame Vestris's production is noteworthy for bringing *Love's Labour's Lost* back to the professional repertoire, with much of it intact: the overhearing scene is back, the Worthies appear, Marcade enters, and the ending alludes to the parting of the four couples. Yet the sense that the men and women were actually separating may not have been clear to the audiences watching this production's spectacular finale. Details from the prompt book (Folger Library, *Love's Labour's Lost* 2) make clear that Madame Vestris staged a large production number. The first verse of the final song ('Spring') begins with a procession: 2 Wild Men carrying clubs; a Huntsman with a pole and bird; 4 Huntsmen with horns; 6 Shepherds and 6 Shepherdesses, each carrying a crook; Flora, a goddess, accompanied by 6 children with wreaths of flowers who then usher in the Emblem of Spring. The second verse ('Winter') brings another procession: 2 more Wild Men; 4 Woodcutters with hatchets, plus log bearers; 4 Winter Shepherds; Dick the Shepherd and Joan the Milkmaid; Lords of Misrule; a Boar's Head; and the Emblem of Winter, drawn on by 2 Boys (representing the winds). There may have been a third verse, for there is certainly a third procession: 4 servants carrying sticks; 6 Pages; 2 Gentlemen with wands; 9 Banners of the Worthies, and then Holofernes, Armado, Sir Nathaniel, Moth, and Costard, followed by an officer and 6 Guards. The prompt book's final stage direction indicates that these processions turned into a kind of curtain call with music: 'All down to the first 8 bars and seperate [sic] right and left, go up and range at back. Pages in front leaving the Worthies in centre.' The King and Princess then enter from the pavilion up centre and pose for the final tableau.

Many of the onstage figures thus presented embody allusions from the songs themselves: the shepherds piping on oaten straws become '6 Shepherds and 6 Shepherdesses' while the 'wreaths of flowers' doubtless contained 'daisies pied and violets blue'; Dick the Shepherd and Joan the Milkmaid are literally from the text; Tom, who 'bears logs into the hall', expands into '4 Woodcutters with hatchets, plus log bearers'. But other figures create an allegorical dimension, with 'Flora, a goddess' and the 'Emblem of Spring' as well as the 'Emblem of Winter'. Winter seems to evoke a representation of Christmas, since the procession includes the Lords of Misrule who traditionally presided over the Twelfth Night festivities, and a 'Boar's Head', often seen at a Christmas feast. Such extravagance may have come from the fertile imagination of James Robinson Planché, who had worked with Madame Vestris from the beginning of her management of the Olympic Theatre some eight years earlier, and who functioned in a variety of capacities: adaptor, literary adviser, costume designer. Perhaps, emboldened by the greater size of Covent Garden, both Planché and Madame Vestris indulged their love of scenic opulence – or, perhaps fearing that the unfamiliar play needed help, they tried to make it look as gorgeous as possible. The introduction of the 'Wild Men' into what has always seemed a highly decorous sylvan setting – lacking even the hungry lioness or the green and gilded snake of the Forest of Arden – reflects Planche's antiquarian leanings; he had published a *History of English Costume* in 1834 and had edited Joseph Strutt's two-volume work, *A Complete View of the Dress and Habits of the People of England* (originally published 1796-99, with Planche's edition appearing in 1842). In Strutt's companion work, *The Sports and Pastimes of the People of England* (1801), he describes figures called variously 'green men', 'woodhouses', and 'wodehouses', all associated with pageants and processions. Small wonder that these creatures, dressed in bark and leaves, appeared at the end of a play which had featured an elaborate pageant, leading an even more elaborate procession.

The extravagance of this ending is, on one level, an extension of the pageantry that marked the entire production. In the production's opening moments four guards, an officer, six pages, two gentlemen in black ('as ushers') and four servants preceded the entrance of the King and his three lords. When the Princess first appeared, she was discovered onstage in her tent, accompanied by four pages, two guards, and a herald, as well as Boyet and her ladies. A march onstage by assorted supers and eight musicians heralded the arrival of the Muscovites. In each case, Madame Vestris made sure that the audience enjoyed elaborate stage pictures and sounds. To illustrate the final songs with extra 'characters' and props helps to create a sense of closure, just as musical comedies frequently end with a song and dance for the entire cast. Moreover, such a staging essentially creates the 'happy ending' that Shakespeare has not written, allowing the audience to revel in the spectacle and, by seeing the King and Princess together, perhaps even to forget that she has told him he must go to 'some forlorn and naked hermitage' (V.ii.790).

If Madame Vestris returned the play to the professional stage, it is, however, Samuel Phelps, as actor–manager at Sadler's Wells, whose 1857 production dominates the nineteenth century. Phelps's production was important in its own right but also as a model for later directors who chose to use his prompt book and thus attempted to reproduce Phelps's effects – and his success. During Phelps's tenure as manager at Sadler's Wells, a theatre which had housed cock-fighting, dancing, pantomimes and burlesques (Allen, p. 77), he produced thirty-one of Shakespeare's plays, and these for an audience often seen as lower-class and boisterous (Allen, p. 78). The most vivid description of the Sadler's Wells audience appears in Charles Dickens's 'Shakspeare and Newgate', from *Household Words*, 4 October 1851, an essay on which Dickens collaborated with R. H. Horne; after some preliminary comments about the necessity of art and his belief that 'a well-conducted Theatre is a good place in which to learn good things', Dickens describes the audience *before* Phelps took over as manager:

> Without, the Theatre, by night, was like the worst part of the worst kind of Fair in the worst kind of town. Within, it was a bear-garden, resounding with foul language, oaths, catcalls, shrieks, yells, blasphemy, obscenity – a truly diabolical clamour. Fights took place anywhere, at any period of the performance. The audience were of course directly addressed in the entertainments. An improving melo-drama, called BARRINGTON THE PICKPOCKET, being then extremely popular at another similar Theatre, a powerful counter-attraction, happily entitled JACK KETCH, was produced here, and received with great approbation. It was in the contemplation of the Management to add the physical stimulus of a pint of porter to the moral refreshments offered to every purchaser of a pit ticket, when the Management collapsed and the Theatre shut up. (Dickens, pp. 345-6).

From this sketch of a theatre management inclined to focus on what Dickens sarcastically calls 'moral refreshments', involving Jack Ketch, the public executioner, and his evocation of an atmosphere of rowdiness and probably drunkenness (the pint of porter seems an unnecessary incentive), Dickens shifts to an enumeration of Phelps's reforms: removing the fish-sellers, the beer-sellers, and babies carried in for free. According to Dickens, Phelps even posted a copy of an Act of Parliament prohibiting the 'use of bad language in any public place' and followed up that silent warning with occasions on which he stopped the performance so that an offender could be removed. By the time Dickens wrote 'Shakspeare and Newgate', Sadler's Wells had noticeably changed:

> We question whether a more sensible audience for a good play could be found anywhere than is to be found at Sadler's Wells.... The pit, which is very capacious, is made very comfortable, and is constantly filled by respectable family visitors. A father sits there with his wife and daughters, as quietly, as easily, as free from all offence, as in his own house. (Dickens, p. 349)

The transformation of the audience from one of loud-mouthed rowdies to one of proper Victorian families must have made the production of a relatively obscure Shakespearean play more plausible, and especially when one thinks back to the angry audience which Madame Vestris's fee changes had created when she opened her season at Covent Garden. Yet the history of production in Sadler's Wells, its location, and the very size of the theatre, raise questions about the suitability of *Love's Labour's Lost* for Sadler's Wells. Reviewers sometimes speak of Sadler's Wells, built in 1765, as 'little' but statistics (Allen, pp. 77-80) show that it held about 2,600 spectators, with about 1,000 of those in the pit, or what we would now call the orchestra/stalls section. Seats in the pit (benches, with backs added to them) were relatively cheap as compared with boxes, and this fact, combined with the impression that one had to travel to get there, generated its status as a 'suburban' rather than 'in town' theatre. The water tanks added to the theatre in the early nineteenth century allowed for spectacular effects with sea-scenes and waterfalls. In a theatre with a reputation for spectacle and melodrama, the audience may have found *Love's Labour's Lost* an unlikely choice. And, as an actor–manager known for his performance in major Shakepearean tragic roles, Phelps could have well brushed aside a play which seemed to offer him no chance for a starring role. But studies of Phelps's productions praise his respect for and attention to the text, careful rehearsals and ensemble acting. These qualities may explain why Phelps would chance a production of Shakespeare's little-performed comedy in 1857.

As Shirley S. Allen's study of Phelps and Sadler's Wells shows (Allen, 1971), Phelps was remarkable among mid-nineteenth-century British actor–managers for his lack of ego, his emphasis on balanced productions, and his return to relatively complete texts of Shakespeare's plays. It was he who finally removed the dancing and singing witches from *Macbeth*, while returning Lady Macduff and even part of the Porter's speech to the play. In his first season at Sadler's Wells, he produced Shakespeare's *Richard III*, rather than Colley Cibber's version, restoring Queen Margaret, Clarence, Stanley and Hastings, just as later he would restore the Induction to *The Taming of the Shrew*. Though Phelps played Hamlet and Richard III in the first season, his willingness to take on lesser roles is noticeable: he was Christopher Sly, he was Bottom, and in *Love's Labour's Lost* he was Don Armado.

Reconstructing Phelps's production from the 1857-58 season is, to a large extent, an exercise in pulling together details both from the prompt book and from what we know about other productions at Sadler's Wells. Theatre spaces had changed greatly since Shakespeare's time, with the move to indoor instead of outdoor theatres involving a number of changes for staging Shakespeare's plays. Instead of a basically bare stage, with actors often wearing costume contemporary with the audience rather than with the period of the play, and performances taking place in mid-afternoon, nineteenth-century theatres featured elaborate sets, historically detailed costumes, and artificial lighting. Reports on Phelps's *Hamlet*, first staged in 1844, indicate that Phelps achieved impressive effects for the entrance of the Ghost by using a series of lighting effects: a dark stage at the beginning, then a moonlit castle upstage, the reflection of the moon, and lighting tracing the disappearance of the Ghost. In 1853, Phelps's production of *A Midsummer Night's Dream* created the 'dream-like' nature of the forest with a 'curtain of green gauze placed between the actors and the audience' (Morley, p. 57); moreover, the moon, to which characters refer so often, appeared not just in the forest scenes, but, as Morley puts it, 'shining on the palace as the curtains are drawn that admit the fairy throng' (Morley, p. 58). Clearly nothing so exotic was needed for *Love's Labour's Lost*, but the production none the less illustrates Phelps's ability to create memorable stage pictures.

For *Love's Labour's Lost*, Phelps used painted backdrops showing 'wooded landscapes' while the courtiers appeared in medieval attire (Allen, p. 246). John Oxenford, reviewing the production for *The Times*, praised the 'charming picture of a mediaeval Court, resting beneath the shade of the greenwood tree, and by the side of the brook' (Phelps and Forbes-Robertson, p. 165). The set for the third act (including Shakespeare's III.i and IV.i) involved some kind of green bank, since at the beginning of III.i Armado is 'discovered' on the bank, listening to Moth singing; Shakespeare's text doesn't tell us what Moth sings, but in Phelps's production Moth strummed a lute and sang 'If that the world of love were young', based on the first verse of Ralegh's 'The Nymph's Reply to the Shepherd'. Of course there was a tree for Berowne in IV.iii; stage directions tell us when he descends from the tree. The last scene included the Princess's pavilion, as in the Madame Vestris production, although it is not clear how much of the stage this pavilion occupied. Given the number of people who have to be on stage for the final scene, one guesses that it was perhaps just a tentlike entrance rather than a free-standing, large tent.

While the scenery earned praise from reviewers, much of the effect of the production seems to have derived from stage pictures created by the actors themselves. The King of Navarre and his friends were accompanied by six lords, while the Princess of France and her women had six lords and six ladies attending them. Stage directions from the prompt book usually instruct these non-speaking characters to 'range at back', implying that audiences always saw each court with its backdrop of servants. The prompt book's notation for the beginning of IV.i is typical: 'Princess, Rosaline, Maria, Katharine, Boyet, and 6 Ladies in Hunting Dresses, also 6 Supers as Hunters.' Doubtless the six lords attending the women in II.i then changed their costumes and reappeared as hunters for this scene. Oxenford's review suggests that not just the scenery, but also 'the costumes and the groupings all carry us back to that atmosphere of sylvan aristocracy of which we may read at large in the *Arcadia* of Sir Philip Sydney' (Phelps and Forbes-Robertson, p. 165).

For the Pageant of the Nine Worthies, Phelps created an elaborate play-within-a-play. From the pavilion '4 Supers bring out 2 seats ... and place them against the wings'. The four young men then lead the ladies to the seats, which suggests that there are eight seats in all, each super carrying out two. Then '2 Green Men draw on platform'; these descendants of Madame Vestris's Wild Men thus create a stage upon the stage. For further spectacle, Phelps added a Banner Bearer for each Worthy. The prompt book refers to a Banner Bearer for Pompey, Alexander, Judas Maccabeus and Hector; did Holofernes consider Moth as the infant Hercules undeserving of one? As the pageant progresses, not only does Sir Nathaniel have to leave the platform in disgrace, but Costard/Pompey even pushes off his Banner Bearer, once it is clear that Nathaniel has 'overthrown Alisander the conqueror'.

After Marcade's entrance, a moment for which there are, unfortunately, no stage directions, the two Green Men take off the platform, while Boyet 'gives directions to the Super Lords to remove the seats', which they do, taking them into the tent. The ending itself bears some resemblance to the one created by Madame Vestris. Phelps limited himself to two processions instead of three, each focusing on a 'car' (chariot), one with Winter on it, the other with Spring. The men and women seem to be upstage, either by the tents or just in front of them, while the two chariots, Armado, Holofernes, Nathaniel, Dull, Costard, and the four Banner Bearers appear. The four verses at the end become just three – a verse for Spring, a verse for Winter, and then a verse for Spring. There is no closing winter verse, nor the last words of Armado.

Instead the orchestra plays a march, while Boyet escorts the Princess downstage, followed by her three women. 'They come down,' says the prompt book, 'and are saluted by King, Biron, Dumaine and Longaville.' If 'salute' means 'kiss,' then the ending seems romantic, countering the text's insistence on separating the couples. But 'salute' could also signify a formal gesture, such as a bow, and that is what the final stage direction suggests: 'as the last couple goes up bowing and curtseying, adieus', and then 'Ring Down curtain'. Where Madame Vestris created a spectacle which in many ways denied the separation of the lovers, Phelps's ending is not only less spectacular but, as the play itself is, more ambiguous. The 'adieus' upstage, followed by the curtain, do imply separation.

Phelps's ending for *Love's Labour's Lost* embodies what seem the major qualities of his production. It was, most noticeably, a production which emphasised the beauty and gracefulness of the characters in a 'series of sparkling pictures' (Phelps and Forbes-Robertson, p. 165). Oxenford suggests that Phelps created this 'display of picturesque beauty and completeness of detail' (p. 164) to compensate for the play's deficiencies, as well as to insure an audience for 'the piece that he designs for the curiosity of the season' (p. 165). The deficiencies Oxenford found in *Love's Labour's Lost* echo familiar complaints: 'the want of definite purpose, the abundance of obsolete pleasantries that are bandied about, and the avowedly unsatisfactory nature of the conclusion' (p. 165). Just as the anonymous adaptor of *The Students* clearly found Shakespeare's ending in need of revision, so Oxenford feels that the play fails as comedy; his praise of Phelps's work thus begins from the premise that the play needs rescuing – and that a good way to rescue it to make the production elegant and beautiful. Even if the play concerns 'the elaboration of trifles' (p. 165) the audience can sit back and enjoy the production's charm and evocation of a courtly, aristocratic world.

But just as the production's ending blended spectacle with careful ambiguity, so too did the production as a whole. The subtlety of Phelps's production is apparent in the detailed commentary reviewers gave to the actors. Phelps, who played Armado, naturally attracted the most commentary. Henry Morley commented on the resemblance between Malvolio and Armado, 'both fantastical and foolish men' and then praised Phelps for defining 'the essential difference between the two' (p. 167). Morley recreates for us the façade of Armado as well as the pathos which Phelps evoked:

[34]

He affects finery of speech, and is so utterly destitute of ideas, that to count three he must depend upon the help of a child who is his servant, and his master in all passages of wit. He carries a brave outside of clothes, but cannot fight in his shirt, because, as he is driven to admit, 'the naked truth of it is, I have no shirt.' This is the view of his character to which Mr. Phelps gives prominence by many a clever touch, such as the empty drawl on the word love, whenever Armado uses it, or the lumbering helplessness of wit displayed by the great Spaniard when magnificently and heavily conversing with the tiny Moth, in which part little Miss Rose Williams has been taught to bring out very perfectly some telling points. (Morley, p. 167)

Oxenford too praises Phelps, but extends his observations to Mr Williams as Holofernes (and, offstage, the father of Rose/Moth), to Mr Ball as Costard, Mr Meagreson as Dull, and then to the courtly figures. Oxenford's review sees the play as one 'over which a great deal of good acting may be diffused, for even the smallest parts are marked characters and some of them very strongly and very strangely defined ... [Mr Phelps] has so well applied the talent of his company that there is not a single weakly acted part' (Phelps and Forbes-Robertson, p. 165). The emphasis on what might be called the 'ensemble' effect of the play and the praise for the director's ability to create a strong company are motifs that will turn up repeatedly in later responses to productions (Holding, *passim*). Similarly, the delight in the comic characters, with attention going first to Armado and Holofernes, while perhaps strange to literary critics, is familiar to theatre audiences. Lines which seem obscure on the page become clear when spoken, as Oxenford's review suggests:

Holofernes, the schoolmaster, a fop of the pedantic sort, as exceptional in his way as Don Adriano, is most carefully and naturally rendered by Mr. Williams, who happily combines the scholastic sensitiveness with a fund of internal good nature. The line, 'boné for bené: Priscian a little scratched; 'twill serve,' he gives with marvellous effect, showing at once the magnitude of the crime committed by the ignorant curate and his own magnanimity in passing it over. (Phelps and Forbes-Robertson, p. 165)

To find not only the pedantry of Holofernes, but the engaging quality of such details, argues an actor of skill and a production which did not condescend either to the characters or to the audience. Dickens suggests that Phelps's efforts were illuminated by 'great intelligence': 'The smallest character has been respectfully approached and studied; the smallest accessory has been well considered; every artist in his degree has been taught to adapt his part, in the complete effect, to all the other parts uniting to make up the whole' (Dickens, p. 348).

As a result, Dickens concludes, 'The management and audience have reacted on each other' (p. 349). Phelps's success in creating, as Dickens noted, both a group of skilful actors and a receptive audience, was crucial to the future stage life of *Love's Labour's Lost*. Madame Vestris's attempt to revive the play might well have killed it since the opening night débâcle was so widely discussed. But after Phelps's production, *Love's Labour's Lost*, passed over for so many years, received both critical and popular welcome and so awoke after a very long sleep.

CHAPTER III

'The scene begins to cloud': Stratford-upon-Avon, 1946

Slowly *Love's Labour's Lost* became part of the professional reper-toire, never again disappearing so completely as it had during the eighteenth century, but still very much a play to be produced occasionally rather than regularly. Though Phelps's production was to prove immensely influential in that later nineteenth-century and early twentieth-century productions would follow his prompt book, the play did not appear on London's professional stage again until 1918 when it was presented at the Old Vic, where it reap-peared in 1923 and again in 1928. In New York, Augustin Daly produced it in 1874 and 1891. In Stratford-upon-Avon, it was staged in 1885 and 1907, and then under the W. Bridges-Adams management, in 1925 and 1934. Though nine years may seem a long time between productions (at Stratford today, the play ap-pears approximately once every five years), it is a much shorter gap than had existed previously: twenty-two years, or eighteen years. In Birmingham, Barry Jackson produced the play at the Birmingham Rep in 1919, a production revived in 1925.

The more the play was performed, the more chance directors and audiences had to see that it was playable, perhaps surprisingly so. George R. Foss, who directed the Old Vic's 1918 production, noted:

> My production was the first time this play had been tried at the Old Vic, and the clientele of this home of Shakespeare seemed to take very kindly to it. They were surprised, I think, to find that it acted so well, and afforded so many good parts for their favourite actors. What had been

[37]

somewhat vague, pedantic and uninteresting to read, became quaint, bright, and amusing when acted. (Foss, p. 152)

Foss's description of the play's effect is significant since it indicates the principal moods that productions of the play would present in the first forty-five years of the twentieth century. Yet gradually, and occasionally, directors and critics found moments that were more than 'quaint, bright, and amusing'. Nugent Monck, founder and director of the amateur Norwich Players, a group which produced all of Shakespeare's plays in the Maddermarket Theatre (an eighteenth-century structure designed originally as a chapel but remodelled into a theatre space approximating the Fortune), recommended using the balcony level for important entrances and exits, and pointed out that in *Love's Labour's Lost* 'a more impressive effect is gained if the messenger of the French King's death stands alone above the gaiety on the middle stage' (Monck, p. 73). Though the context of Monck's remarks indicates that he is focusing primarily on a physical description of the Maddermarket stage and how it might be used in producing Shakespeare's plays, his example gives us a suddenly vivid picture of Marcade's entrance: gaiety below, solemnity above. And a June 1924 production by the Oxford University Drama Society (OUDS), working under the direction of H. K. Ayliff from the Birmingham Rep, also seemed to focus on the moment of Marcade's entrance. Robert Speaight, then an Oxford undergraduate, saw the production from his vantage point as Assistant [Stage] Manager:

> It [Marcade's entrance] should be a long entrance, with all eyes turned towards it. In Wadham gardens the June night was falling and the projectors were beginning to light up the greensward and to catch the wrinkled bark of the trees. Emlyn Williams was playing Dull and Veronica Turleigh was the Rosaline. Then, all of a sudden, out of the deep and very distant shadows a magnificent figure in black came striding. There was a great sweeping bow – Gyles Isham knew how to bow … .(Speaight, p. 70)

Though we know little else about Monck's production or Ayliff's, we can clearly see how each director recognised the importance of Marcade's entrance. Both interpretations seemed primarily cheerful but both also emphasised, however briefly, this entrance's chilling effect.

On the professional stage, Tyrone Guthrie's production of *Love's Labour's Lost* in 1932 at the Westminster Theatre took its cue from Monck's amateur production; indeed, Guthrie acknowledged that 'most of the good ideas in my production were culled from Monck's at Norwich' (Guthrie, p. 84). Guthrie appreciated Monck's use of a permanent set, which meant 'there were no breaks between scenes' (p. 84), as well as the simple and sympathetic treatment of the comic episodes. Of course Guthrie added his own sense of the style of the play. He cut the text drastically and played it at top speed; ninety minutes seems extremely short. His 1932 production was seen by Harcourt Williams, then director of the Old Vic, who, on the basis of what he saw, recommended Guthrie to Lilian Baylis. In 1936, Guthrie restaged *Love's Labour's Lost* at the Old Vic, in a production characterised by 'an iridescent lightness that kept the wit buoyant, mobile as quicksilver' (Williamson, p. 58). But Guthrie also managed to convey a bittersweet mood when Marcade entered, and even more at the end when 'Moth sang his final song in a twilight illumined by the glow of torches' (Williamson, p. 58). The shift from the 'grand finale' spectacles of Madame Vestris and Samuel Phelps is noticeable; the last moments are not a triumphant climax, but something more like a 'dying fall'. Though Guthrie evidently staged the last two songs with Costard as Winter and Moth as Spring, it was the young Gordon Miller's sweet voice which reviewers remembered. As Williamson put it, 'we leave the theatre with Moth's song of Spring and Winter, and Armado's brief strange epilogue, ringing plaintively in our ears' (p. 57).

The melancholy tone implicit in Guthrie's approach to the ending is particularly striking in view of his formalised setting and almost dancelike blocking. The 1932 production had, according to Gordon Crosse, just one set, 'with the king's pavilion draped in red on one side and the Princess's in green on the other, each group of characters dressed in the corresponding colour and keeping strictly to its own side in all entrances and exits' (p. 94). Such precision echoes Monck's rule that 'if the place remains unchanged, the characters should come in and go out on the same side' (Monck, p. 73). By the time Guthrie revived the production in 1936, the colour scheme had shifted noticeably, with Audrey Williamson praising Molly MacArthur's 'costumes in pastel shades of pink, green and cream against a delicate scene which comprised only a fountain, two tents on either side of the stage, and a wrought iron gate, topped by an arc of fresh leaves, leading into the domains of Navarre'. The set, one notes, seems essentially the same, but the softening of the colour scheme (assuming Crosse's description is accurate) may indicate that Guthrie saw a more mellow, less brit-

[39]

tle, world than in his earlier version, one into which the 'plaintive' notes of the end would fit more easily.

Guthrie's cast was young, and full of actors who would later become better known. Alec Clunes played Berowne, and Michael Redgrave played Navarre, while Redgrave's wife, Rachel Kempson, played the Princess and Margaretta Scott was 'the dark and taunting Rosaline' (Williamson, p. 56). In between Osrics (to John Gielgud's Hamlet in 1934 and to Laurence Olivier's in 1936) Alec Guinness, with a trim Vandyke beard and small but swirling moustache, played Boyet – an accident of casting which reminds us of Berowne's description of Boyet as 'wit's pedlar' and 'the ape of form, monsieur the nice' (V.ii. 317, 324). And in a change from the prevailing tradition of petite actresses cast as Moth (Joan White played the part in 1932 and in 1934 Patricia Hayes at Stratford played Moth for W. Bridges-Adams), Guthrie cast Gordon Miller, who would go on to play Puck. The senior actor of the group was Ernest Milton, who played Armado primarily at the level of parody, but 'did not fail to reveal the man's rather touching pride in poverty at the last' (Williamson, p. 58).

The power of Guthrie's production, in all its elements, both lighthearted and sombre, is evident from John Dover Wilson's chapter, 'Love's Labour's Lost: The Story of a Conversion', in *Shakespeare's Happy Comedies* (1962). Wilson had edited the play for the Cambridge Shakespeare in 1923 and spent most of the introduction chasing topical references. But after seeing Guthrie's 1936 production, he confesses: 'Mr. Guthrie not only gave me a new play, the existence of which I had never suspected, which indeed had been veiled from men's eyes for three centuries, but he set me at a fresh standpoint of understanding and appreciation from which the whole of Shakespearian comedy might be reviewed in a new light' (p. 64). Wilson announces that he will discuss the play 'from the point of view of a spectator, not from that of an editor' (p. 65), and his comments on pace and rhythm, on pattern, on the 'constantly changing' colour-scheme, all reflect the masterful variety of Guthrie's production. Wilson then comes to the ending:

> The extraordinary impression left upon the audience by the entrance of the black-clad messenger upon the court revels was the greatest lesson I took away with me from the Guthrie production. It made me see two things – (a) that however gay, however riotous a Shakespearian comedy may be, tragedy is always there, *felt*, if not seen; (b) that for all its surface lightness and frivolity, the play had behind it a serious mind at work, with a purpose. (p.73)

[40]

Despite this heartfelt testimonial, Wilson's concluding pages do not offer a clear sense of how one might move from generalisations about tragedy and purpose to a more specific analysis of the play; instead he talks about the 'eternal type of pedant' (Holofernes) against whom Shakespeare 'hoists the banner of Love' (pp. 73-4). And while Wilson may have felt a new understanding of *Love's Labour's Lost* in 1936, he did not make such views clear in his writing for almost thirty years. The change in tone, suggested by Monck and Guthrie, finally became emphatic in 1946 when Peter Brook's production (so successful that it was immediately revived for the 1947 season) emphasised the play's darker aspects with such clarity that future productions would recognise them and future scholarship would find the 'new play' to which Wilson alludes. Though Brook's comments on his production never mention the Second World War directly, it seems only plausible that his sensitivity to the play's potential for tragedy may have grown out of that great conflict.

The other major context for Brook's production was domestic and theatrical, but still complex. Even before the war made theatrical productions more difficult to cast and stage, productions at Stratford had come to seem stagnant:

> One of the most remarkable things about the Diamond Jubilee season [1939] and the Memorial's productions generally after sixty years of existence was the predictability of its directorial vision, which hampered even the most talented of its actors. It could be seen most clearly in the staging of the plays, in the use of debased Edwardian-style sets, in the fustian and conventional costuming, in the waxwork groups of supers. But it was not just the staging which had fossilized; the playing of certain scenes, the conceptions of many characters, even decisions about the texts, once taken, remained sacrosanct. (Beauman, p. 159)

Beauman offers the chilling example of *A Midsummer Night's Dream*, staged five times between 1937 and 1944, with sets and costumes, in increasingly poor condition, taken from a 1932 production. Yet since the season continued to make money, change was slow in coming.

By 1946, after three different artistic directors had resigned (in 1942, 1943, and 1945), Stratford-upon-Avon desperately needed change; as one might expect, such change inevitably created controversy. Sir Barry Jackson, best known for his work at the Birmingham Repertory Theatre where H. K. Ayliff had directed a modern-dress *Hamlet* in 1925, took over as artistic director. For this first post-war season, Jackson decided to create a new company at Stratford with entirely new actors. None of the actors he hired had ever appeared at Stratford before, and many of them were relatively new to Shakespeare, including Valerie Taylor who, though well known in London, would play her first professional Shakespearean roles as Imogen, Lady Macbeth and the Princess of France. Jackson wanted not only a fresh start in terms of actors but also a new approach to scheduling, and so decided that only three plays would open at first, after a ten-week rehearsal period, and that the remaining five plays would open over the next three months, each with a three-week rehearsal period, dubbed a 'Stratford innovation' (*Yorkshire Post*, 22 January 1946). The 1946 schedule, with three performances of *The Tempest* followed by three performances of *Cymbeline* all between April 20 and April 25, suggests just how crowded even the new schedule was. Though Jackson promised no startling or revolutionary productions and certainly nothing in modern dress, his decision to give the actors more rehearsal time created opposition from playgoers accustomed to seeing four plays in three days.

Even more controversy arose that year at the annual meeting of the Board of Governors on the morning of the traditional Shakespeare's birthday celebrations, Tuesday 23 April. The governors faced a proposal from Captain A. S. Cunningham-Reid that four members of the board should be replaced with the view of creating an executive council that would insist on recruiting more stars for the Stratford season. Barry Jackson both defended his actors and pointed out that the economic reality created by the film industry made it impossible for him to get actors such as Olivier and Richardson (whom, he said, he had asked) to leave London where they could act in films during the day and on stage at night. Finally Jackson and Colonel Fordham Flower, the chairman of the Board of Governors, issued a statement arguing that they gave priority to 'quality' rather than to 'financial considerations', that they had invited 'experienced actors of repute' in Robert Harris and Valerie Taylor, that they wanted Stratford to 'encourage the young and promising actor' and that Cunningham-Reid had made an 'uninformed assertion' (*The Times*, 25 April 1946). Such discussion of 'stars' and Stratford still occurs today, but it is interesting to notice such an argument at the beginning of the season that included *Love's Labour's Lost*, a play which seems to offer little to such stars – and which may, indeed, benefit, as Samuel Phelps had shown, from sustained ensemble playing.

If many of Jackson's decisions caused consternation and extended comment in both local and national newspapers, at least the choice to invite not just new actors but also new directors turned out to be a major success. Peter Brook was just twenty years old when Barry Jackson invited him to Stratford to direct *Love's Labour's Lost*; as an Oxford undergraduate Brook had filmed a version of Sterne's *A Sentimental Journey*; and, without any major professional theatrical experience, he had directed three plays at the Birmingham Rep, Shaw's *Man and Superman*, Shakespeare's *King John* (with a young Paul Scofield playing John Tanner and then the Bastard), and Ibsen's *Lady from the Sea*. Jackson must have trusted Brook's instincts completely because he entrusted him with what J. C. Trewin calls '[Jackson's] most prized comedy' (Trewin, 1963, p. 58). Despite his intensive work at the Rep and despite the absence of well-known actors who might look down on him, Brook clearly felt anxious about his 'first big production' and thus spent a great deal of time preparing for his first rehearsal:

> I sat agonized in front of a model of the set, aware that further hesitation would soon be fatal, fingering folded pieces of cardboard – forty pieces representing the forty actors to whom the following morning I would have to give orders, definite and clear. Again and again, I staged the very first entry of the Court, recognizing that this was when all would be lost or won, numbering the figures, drawing charts, manoeuvring the scraps of cardboard to and fro, on and off the set, trying them in big batches, then in small, from the side, from the back, over grass mounds, down steps, knocking them all over with my sleeve, cursing and starting again. As I did so, I noted the moves, and with no one to notice my indecision, crossed them out, then made fresh notes. The next morning I arrived at rehearsal, a fat prompt-book under my arm, and the stage management brought me a table, reacting to my volume, I observed, with respect. (*The Empty Space*, pp. 119-20)

Brook's worries may have sprung from his youth, his comparative lack of experience, his awareness of Stratford's reputation – as well as the play's own insistent formality. Fortunately, for Brook and for the production, he immediately recognised that his detailed, almost military, planning was useless, since the actors 'were not remotely like my cardboard figures, these large human beings thrusting themselves forward, some too fast with lively steps I had not foreseen, bringing them suddenly on top of me'. At that moment, he realised (though he did not write about it for some time), 'my whole future work hung in the balance. I stopped and walked away from my book, in amongst the actors, and I have never looked at a written plan since' (*The Empty Space*, p. 120).

In a later collection of essays, *The Shifting Point*, Brook makes clear that his approach to *Love's Labour's Lost* was much more than a frenzied attempt to block the play, but stemmed rather from his initial, intuitive response, 'a deep, formless hunch which is like a smell, a colour, a shadow' (p. 3). And the key to Brook's hunch about *Love's Labour's Lost* came from two sources, the text of the play and the paintings of Jean-Antoine Watteau (1684-1721):

> When I studied the text of *Love's Labour's Lost*, I was struck by something that seemed to me to be self-evident, but which at the time seemed to be unheard of: that when, at the very end of the last scene, a new, unexpected character called Mercade (sic) came on, the whole play changed its tone entirely. He came into an artificial world to announce a piece of news that was real. He came on bringing death. And as I felt intuitively that the image of the Watteau world was very close to this, I began to see that the reason that the Watteau *Age of Gold* is so particularly moving is that although it's a picture of springtime, it's an autumn springtime, because every one of Watteau's pictures has an incredible melancholy. And if one looks, one sees that there is somewhere in it the presence of death, until one even sees that in Watteau (unlike the imitations of the period, where it's all sweetness and prettiness) there is usually a dark figure somewhere, standing with his back to you, and some people say that he is Watteau himself. But there's no doubt that the dark touch gives the dimension to the whole piece. (*The Shifting Point*, p. 11).

Although Brook's implication that it was 'unheard of' for directors to notice the change of tone in the play seems to ignore moments from Guthrie's 1932 and 1936 productions, his 'intuitive' feeling that the paintings of Watteau furnished a visual image corresponding to the play's verbal images *and* that the image was one of 'an autumn springtime' with 'incredible melancholy' represents a major shift in the approach to the play. Brook refers to Watteau's *Age of Gold*, but his production explicitly 'quotes' two other paintings. The stage set for 'the Garden' (used for II.i, III.i, IV.i and V.ii) shows a huge urn looming over the characters in a position similar to the urn in *Fête vénitienne* (see Figures I and II). The white costume worn by the mesmerising and poignant *Gilles* in Watteau's painting of a group of actors turns up twice in Brook's production, both for Costard and for the silent figure added by Brook, the 'zany' attending the Princess (in Figure II, he sits at the bottom of the staircase). And several critics referred to Watteau's large-scale canvas, *Voyage á Cythère*, with its groups of fashionable lovers in a wooded setting, as a reference point for the overall look of the production. Using Watteau's paintings as the inspiration for stage sets and costumes was not a completely new idea; in 1936, Molly MacArthur designed

As You Like It for the Old Vic (Edith Evans as Rosalind) with 'scenes and costumes *á la Watteau*' (Byrne, p. 16). The design choice solved the problem of the pastoral convention 'by setting the play in the period which, because of Watteau's pictures, is, above all others, associated in people's minds with this particular form of artificiality' (Byrne, p. 16). Perhaps some such thoughts occurred to Brook as he began to work on *Love's Labour's Lost*, a play even more full of convention and artifice than *As You Like It*; while the banished courtiers in Arden notice the cold weather, the characters in *Love's Labour's Lost* never seem aware of 'the penalty of Adam'. Even the Princess's sarcastic reply to the King's welcome, 'the roof of this court is too high to be yours, and welcome to the wide fields too base to be mine' (II.i.92-3), seems a complaint for effect rather than because she genuinely feels uncomfortable. The use of paintings as the inspiration for stage sets and costumes returns frequently in twentieth-century productions of *Love's Labour's Lost*, and Brook's successful production may have been the beginning of that trend.

While in certain particulars the set and costumes by Reginald Leefe echoed the paintings of Watteau and his contemporary Nicolas Lancret (1690-1743), they also defined their own deliberately theatrical and artificial world. On the stage floor a platform about six inches high, with small white posts around its perimeter and a white rope linking the posts, created a stage-within-a-stage. Two symmetrical structures flanked the stage, each with a curtained doorway, topped by a narrow balcony and a curtained and diamond-grilled window; since the doorway and the window were the same size, the symmetry was pronounced. Between these 'houses', which formed a kind of proscenium within the theatre's existing proscenium arch, specially-created act curtains appeared at the beginning of each of Brook's three acts. The performance began with a mime-prologue, and a view of the first stage curtain, which featured a castle entrance, with a huge door, a giant lock, and printed on the curtain the opening of the King's edict: 'Proclamation. Item. That no woman shall come within a mile of my court.' The two towers flanking that door created yet another inner proscenium and the sense of a world closing in on itself. As the lights came up the audience saw four women – not the Princess and her group, but four whores (also identified as 'four Spanish ladies' in the 1947 prompt book), clearly a challenge to the writing behind them. Constable Dull entered to the sound of a crashing cymbal, symbolically suggesting male authority vs. female sexuality; does

[45]

Dull's foolishness thus extend to the King he serves? J. C. Trewin speaks of the 'dumb-show prologue in which Navarre's tearful women read the King's ungallant proclamation' (*Peter Brook*, p. 26) while Audrey Williamson speaks of 'a ballet of sluts shaking their fists at Navarre's proclamation' (Williamson, p. 58); but whatever their attitude, the women exited, chased off by Dull.

After the prologue, a blackout, and stage lights up again, the 'Proclamation' curtain disappeared to reveal yet another stage, with two steps up to the main platform, and a set of steps, one rectangular and one curved, leading offstage right. A huge metal globe on a small table–bench represented the study, while behind the platform a series of arches gracefully yet lightly indicated the interior of the palace. A small tentlike covering to the arches at the top of the first set of stairs created yet one more space-within-a-space, and here the King first appeared, looking through the telescope attached to one of the posts. Thus the series of inset stages, from the main stage to the roped-off platform, to the stage revealed behind the curtain, to the small 'pavilion', framed an increasingly artificial world. The stylised setting both reminds the audience that it is watching a play and comments on that play; clearly very little *real* study would take place in such a theatricalised space.

The main set for the production, the 'Garden' in which most of the action takes place, was equally artificial. With little greenery (a few trees far upstage right) and a mound right of centre, it was clearly more like a patio, with a huge flight of stairs sweeping in from up left, the Watteau urn prominently displayed on the stair column, and the two side structures creating the sense of the palace nearby. For the first scene involving Holofernes, Nathaniel, and Dull (IV.ii), Brook returned the action to the first set, the King's study; their second scene (V.i) began after the second interval with another special drop curtain, this one showing cartoon versions of Holofernes, Nathaniel and Dull peering through a huge telescope (called a periscope in the prompt book). The centre of the painted telescope was actually another curtain, or 'blind', which lifted to reveal a table with the remains of a banquet, and Dull collapsed in sleep at the table. Once again, Brook presented a stage-within-a-stage, this time complicating the effect so that painted versions of the characters seem to look at their 'real-life' counterparts acting within the space of the telescope's lens. Moreover, since the first scene showed the King looking through a small telescope, the drop curtain suggested that the watchers might well become the watched, a reversal of roles appropriate to the final scene in which the men who originally vowed not to talk to women for three years now must beg for the women's love.

Although the use of two major sets might seem at first to slow down the production by requiring time for set changes, Brook's designer placed these sets on slip stages so that they could slide in and out behind curtains, and thereby avoid the break in action caused by a set change; the slip stages were especially important since Brook's division of the play into three sections did not always coincide with set changes. The play's first three scenes, introducing the King's court, Armado and Moth, and the Princess's court formed the first act, and included both the palace-study and garden sets. So did the second act which began with Armado and Moth in the garden, thus focusing even more attention on the melancholy Spaniard. The act ended with Berowne's long speech in IV.iii and a tableau: 'The King places hands on shoulders of others. Slow curtain.' The final shift between palace and garden came during the interval between IV.iii and V.i with the telescope cloth concealing the garden set during the playing of V.i. Then, as Moth climbed on the table to dance in anticipation of the Pageant, Holofernes pulled down the blind, lights went to black, the telescope cloth lifted, the stools and table were cleared, and the immense staircase of the garden reappeared.

Brook's choice to avoid any kind of 'real' forest or park, especially for the great overhearing scene, struck one reviewer as particularly strange, so much so that he included it in a chapter called 'Eccentricities' in his *Shakespearean Playgoing 1890-1952*. Gordon Crosse objected that 'in IV.iii the listeners hid in curtained boxes, a very incongruous feature of a Royal Park' (p. 99). Brook's choice is certainly debatable, but by returning the men to the first set, he emphasised the irony of the men breaking their oath in the very same place where they had originally signed the oath. Almost forty years later, the BBC production would make exactly the same choice, beginning the play in a library and using a set of circular library stairs for Berowne to climb in IV.iii rather than a tree.

The costume choices involved a different kind of artificiality, since they represented not just the different social classes in the play, but a variety of visual and dramatic traditions. The opulent and exquisite eighteenth-century ruffled and trimmed dresses of the French court came from Watteau; Holofernes' fantastically scalloped robe and his exaggerated makeup suggested *commedia dell'arte* just as Costard's white silk outfit not only echoed Watteau's *Gilles* but the traditional Pierrot costume; Dull's policeman's uniform, in light blue, with wide striped cuffs, a truncheon, Victorian helmet and a string of sausages placed him in the nineteenth century, blending a Punch and Judy prop with a costume that might have come from a D'Oyly Carte production of *The Pirates of Penzance*. The rich darkness of Don Armado's costume, with military braid down the front of his jacket, a broad sash, a plumed hat, and a cape, together with the melancholy demeanour of Paul Scofield, suggested Velásquez, while Moth's light-colored costume, trimmed with bold stripes, together with a hat whose shape and plume echoed his master's, combined the Spanish and Italian traditions. Overall this was an affluent society, even though Armado's elaborate costume concealed his true poverty, 'The naked truth of it is, I have no shirt' (V.ii.706). But it was also an amazingly heterogeneous society, one blending the elegance of eighteenth-century France with the modern impudence of Costard's water pistol in the comic battle between him and Armado in the final scene. When Brook wrote later that he 'dressed the character called Constable Dull as a Victorian policeman because his name at once conjured up the typical figure of the London bobby', he added that 'no one was conscious of an anachronism' because, as Brook put it, 'consistency had no relation to real Shakespearian style' (*The Empty Space*, p. 76).

Such inconsistencies are far more common today than they were in 1946, and one of the lasting effects of this Brook production was to establish such eclecticism as a visual shorthand for differentiating character types,.class status, or even moral values. Brook's comment about Dull, for instance, makes clear that he saw Dull as a 'type' rather than an individual; similarly, the costumes for Holofernes and Nathaniel derive from a dramatic form that emphasises 'type' characters. The evidence from both texts of the play (Quarto and Folio) shows that Shakespeare also thought of these characters generically, giving them speech-headings of Constable, Pedant, Curate, etc. But though one could think of Armado as 'Braggart', the speech-heading that turns up at moments in both texts, his character resonates with echoes of Don Quixote; thus the more 'realistic' costume subtly differentiated him from the other comic characters. The larger motivation behind Brook's deliberate inconsistencies, as he made clear in *The Empty Space*, is his perception that Shakespeare's plays constantly shift verbal as well as

[48]

emotional styles, and a non-realistic, even 'inconsistent', design concept may serve to make that variety possible.

Just as the set and the costumes created a world which stressed artifice and elegance, so the patterned movement on the stage reflected the elaborate patterning of Watteau's paintings (cf. Levey, pp. 57-82). When, for example, Boyet read aloud Armado's letter from IV.i and moved first downstage with it and then upstage, the women swirled after him, looking over his shoulder. The dialogue between Boyet and Rosaline (also in IV.i) about the suitor/shooter (a pun lost by Brook's changing of both nouns to 'hunter') became a stylised and choreographed fight; Rosaline aimed her bow and arrow at Boyet and backed him around in a circle, then Boyet changed direction and forced her to back around the stage. The staircase in the garden setting which was used for II.i, III.i, IV.i and V.ii immediately created formal stage pictures which included casual touches, such as the zany sitting on the lowest step; it also served as the 'stage' for the Pageant of the Nine Worthies.

Against this elegance and formality Brook set slapstick humour. Not only did Dull dress differently from the Watteau-like court, but he acted as if he were in a world apart from Watteau's elegant society. Dull led Costard into the first scene on a leash and then tied him to a pillar. When Dull exited to deliver Costard to Armado, he cut off Costard's non-stop cheerfulness by bopping him on the head with his truncheon. During V.i, the 'telescope scene', Dull fell asleep with his head on the table, and had to be woken up by Holofernes; his silence – and his lack of understanding – became even more vivid. And in the Pageant of the Nine Worthies, after Holofernes' abortive attempt at Judas Maccabeus, Dull made an unscripted – and sleeping – appearance, carried in on a litter and draped with a cloth bearing the inscription 'Julius Caesar'. He did wake up in time to strike a pose, but before he could utter any words (there are, of course, none for him in the text), Moth whistled the litter-bearers offstage!

The Pageant of the Nine Worthies always invites comic invention, and Brook's production was particularly rich in these touches. Holofernes presided over the festivities as bell-ringer, and Armado offered the King a programme. After the King read the programme, the National Anthem was played, and then Pompey appeared, though without his traditional 'libbard's head on knee' (V.ii.542), since the prompt book changes that line. Pompey's conclusion, 'And lay my arms before the legs of this sweet lass of France' (V.ii.550), was followed by silence until he knelt and prompted the

[49]

Princess, 'If your ladyship would say "Thanks, Pompey", I had done' (V.ii.551), and the Princess led the applause. But of course it was the appearance of the 'o'erparted' Sir Nathaniel that really began the slapstick comedy. Not only did Nathaniel forget his lines after getting through his first sentence, 'When in the world I lived, I was the world's commander' (V.ii.558), and try to leave the stage (Holofernes had to bring him back), but he raised the placard/scutcheon proudly naming him, 'My scutcheon plain declares that I am Alisander' (V.ii.560), only to be greeted with loud laughter since the placard read 'Nathaniel'. He turned it over, to reveal 'Alisander' and got a round of applause. Just as Holofernes had to lead on the terrified curate, so Costard had to take away the thoroughly embarrassed Nathaniel. Then Moth made the most of his short appearance, hissing for the serpents, taking a bow centre stage, with Holofernes finally chasing him off.

The tone shifted from good-natured comedy to meaner-spirited teasing, with the young men first surrounding Holofernes/Judas on the steps and closing in on him as they interrupted his lines, and then laughing at his discomfiture as he collected the prompt book and left, his rebuke, 'This is not generous, not gentle, not humble' (V.ii.623), prompting a laugh from the onlookers. The appearance of Dull as the sleeping Caesar followed by Armado/Hector circling the stage to show himself off seems to have restored a tone of good, if silly, humour, and the appearance of Costard rushing in, followed by Moth, to break up Armado's speech began to increase the physical comedy of the scene. Armado's threat to Costard, 'Thou shalt die' (V.ii.671), drew murmurs from the crowd, as the watching nobility rose (in anticipation or anxiety?) and attendants cleared away the stools on which the courtiers had sat. Once Moth revealed that Armado cherished Jaquenetta's 'dishclout', the preparations for the fight began: Costard practised warming-up exercises, aimed a water pistol on Armado, was chased by Armado and finally produced Pompey's sword to use for the fight. Armado went up the steps, chased by Costard, and then the duelling pair fought their way down the stairs; attention moved down centre, and slightly left, at the base of the steps where Armado and Costard were fighting while the rest of the cast had spread out to give the combatants room.

Thus, when Marcade entered from up centre, coming over the mound, he was virtually unnoticed, although as he moved down centre, space cleared around him; the 1947 prompt book reads 'dead silence & still'. It was this moment which would be remembered as crucial to the play, and of course, it was with this moment that Brook's 'deep, formless hunch' had begun. In the director's words, 'The man in black came onto a very pretty summery stage, with everybody in pale pastel Watteau and Lancret costumes and golden lights dying. It was very disturbing and at once the whole audience felt that the world had been transformed' (*The Shifting Point*, p. 12). J. C. Trewin's description puts the contrast in terms of weather: 'the company remained stricken into absolute stillness, a fall of frost in the summer night, in the context both daring and just' (*Peter Brook*, p. 26). Certainly the stillness, the creation of space around Marcade, and the gradual drifting away of the trumpeters and lords and ladies contributed to the 'fall of frost'. But even earlier, when Costard had embarrassed Armado by revealing Jaquenetta's pregnancy – 'She's quick; the child brags in her belly already. 'Tis yours' (V.ii.668-9) – the lighting cue reads significantly, 'Fade stars.' So it was on to a darkening stage, albeit one swirling with action, that Marcade entered silently, and it was the combination of exaggerated, even slapstick fighting and sudden silence which created the 'dark touch [which] gives the dimension to the whole piece'.

So effectively did this moment transform the audience's sense of the play that the next major professional staging, Hugh Hunt's 1949 production of *Love's Labour's Lost* for the Old Vic (at the New Theatre), seemed almost by necessity to echo Brook's. Hunt saw the play as a 'comedy of youth', as one which needed 'to satirize insincerity', but primarily as one in which 'this light, seemingly pointless but endlessly charming age of make-belief (sic) has now to face reality' (Hunt, p. 26, p. 7-8); the move from 'make-believe' to 'reality' reminds us of Brook's 'artificial world' and 'death'. Like Brook he divided the play into three movements, although he placed the second interval after V.i rather than after IV.iii, thus leaving the long last scene as the final movement. Unlike Brook, he used a different set for each movement, and arranged for set changes during the intervals. Hunt imagined the castle of Navarre set on 'an island in the middle of a lake, a fact which will preserve its remoteness. Around the lake is the forest or extensive park famous for its deer' (p. 11). Hunt's description of the scenes shows a move into the forest and then out again, with Part I set 'in the most civilized part of the park' (p. 11), complete with 'masonry in the form of temples and statues' artfully arranged 'to provide good vistas from the palace gardens' (p.11). The effect, as Hunt notes, was of 'the forest of Fontainebleau and the park of Versailles' (p.

[51]

11), both noted pleasure-palaces for French kings. The lake was visible throughout, and across the lake, the palace itself. Hunt utilised the lake at first for the arrival of Armado and Moth, landing 'from a boat in which they have been fishing' (p. 12), but most memorably for Marcade's arrival and then for the departure of the Princess. His own description of the ending is worth quoting at length:

> The last movement of this comedy of youth, when the great barge with its black flag, bearing the sorrowful Princess and her leader, moved slowly away to the accompaniment of the song of spring, the gradual darkness shrouding the silhouette of Don Armado, the falling of a leaf from the summer trees, produced a sense of reverence in us all as we stood around in the wings, waiting for those strange enigmatic words, so charged with emotion, 'You that way; we, this way.' An owl hooted and the curtain fell. (p. 26)

Though Hunt contrived what must have been a long entrance for Marcade, in contrast to his sudden appearance in Brook's production, the sense of melancholy from both productions is clear. The closing moments of Hunt's production emphasise separation and death, with the barge, the falling leaf, and 'the melancholy hoot of the owl'. The use of the lake over which 'loomed the barge that brings the funereal Marcade', wrote Richard David, 'was overwhelmingly successful, as was the quiet recapitulation of the lovers' problems that follows, and the final fading of the play in trills and falling darkness' (*Shakespeare Survey*, p. 131).

The quiet of Hunt's ending offered another contrast to Brook's production, for in the final moments, Brook brought on not just the rustics but extra singers as well: four women (representing, according to the 1947 prompt book, Daisy, Violet, Spring, Cuckoobud) and five men (Cuckoo, Snowman, Tom, Fire, and Winter) as well as Holofernes, Sir Nathaniel, and Costard. It is not, of course, a spectacle as elaborate as those of Madame Vestris or Samuel Phelps, but it does suggest that the 'two learned men' have been hard at work, not merely compiling the dialogue but getting a number of costumes ready as well. But if such costuming (implied by the names given to the singers) suggests a certain amount of spectacle, one should note that Brook cut the second verse of the song, so the balance (reversing Phelps) is one verse for Spring and two verses for Winter. He also gave the last lines of the play – 'The words of Mercury are harsh after the songs of Apollo. You that way; we this way' – to the Princess, so that they became words of farewell. The Princess and her women exited up the steps and out, the singers in two lines on the other side of the stage continued to sing, the men stood at the bottom of the staircase gazing after the departing women, and the curtain fell very slowly. In 1947, when the successful production was revived, these last words seem to have been moved slightly earlier in the text so that the Princess spoke them before the last verse of the song, and presumably exited while the final – wintry – verse was sung. This ending, like Brook's entire production, blends many moods – the harmony of the singers, the darkness of the stage, the formal tableau of the young men, together as they were at the beginning, but, we assume, changed. It is a Watteau setting, but without his couples, emphasising, as Berowne does, 'Jack hath not Jill.'

The influence of Brook's production on subsequent productions manifested itself primarily in two ways. First of all, as Hunt's work with the Old Vic Company just three years later makes clear, the darkness of the play's ending became something one could not easily avoid – and which, handled with finesse, became for audiences and critics the most memorable part of the evening. Indeed, just as Paul Scofield made Armado's brooding melancholy not merely funny but engaging, so the ending's evocation of the darker tones of the play recurred frequently. And, as the sixth chapter of this study will show, Brook's insight about the ending seems to lead ultimately to John Barton's work on the play in a 1978 production which began, as well as ended, with autumn leaves.

Secondly, the use of painterly backgrounds for this play occurred more and more often. Richard David describes the backcloth for Hunt's production in terms of 'the backgrounds to Elizabethan miniatures, the more extended works of Hillyard or of Oliver' (p. 130). Brook's production is the obvious ancestor of the 1984 BBC television production where the director again cited Watteau as one of the primary influences. The two most recent productions at Stratford-upon-Avon, Barry Kyle's in 1984 and Terry Hands's in 1990, have used French paintings as the central design concept, both featuring nineteenth-century settings which evoke Impressionist paintings. The 1990 illustrated programme even reproduced two famous works, Manet's 'Déjeuner sur l'Herbe', and Monet's 'Le Déjeuner sur l'herbe', and Timothy O'Brien's design for the production's first moments specifically echoed the Monet painting, with centre stage occupied by a huge blanket–tablecloth, covered with food – a basket of fruit down left, various

[53]

pieces of bread, cheese, wine bottles. Gorgeous cushions are spread around for the young men to lounge on, and the costumes, especially the elegant grey suit with a top hat that Dumaine wears, remind us of the gentlemen in Monet's painting. Manet's painting, in which a naked woman sits with the fully dressed men, is subtly present as well. When the king proposes the oath which outlaws women, the audience may recognise in Manet's work the world which the men try to exclude. Bob Crowley's set for the 1984 production is less explicitly connected to particular paintings, but the costumes are clearly late nineteenth or early twentieth century, with Boyet looking rather like Oscar Wilde. After the first scene, set in the King's richly furnished Edwardian library, complete with four desks, maps, an anatomy chart, and bookcases, the rest of the play takes place in a park dominated by a white floorcloth covered with beige leaves, tall thin poles which blossom into parasols, and behind them, upstage, shadowy trees.

Both productions also feature an artist *manqué*, since in 1990 Longaville is sketching away during the ten minutes preceding the beginning of the play, while in 1984, Berowne is himself the artist. In fact, Roger Rees, who played Berowne, originally trained as an artist, and he carried a sketch pad with him in his first two scenes (I.i and II.i). Carrying the joke to its logical extreme, Berowne gave Rosaline a huge portrait of himself for the 'favour'; in that painting, a semi-nude Berowne stood with a cloth draped over one shoulder, the other one bare, and his bare arm draped with a necklace.

The development of painterly allusions in sets and costumes reflects more than just a wish to find an appropriate decor, French or English, for the play. The use of Watteau and Lancret, Monet and Manet, evokes a world of elegance and ease, one in which people have time to amuse themselves. Creating that elegant world, first to make clear that these are people who can afford to lounge about, enjoying their own wit, and then to break through the artificiality has become a familiar strategy for directors of *Love's Labour's Lost*. One might even argue that just as a painting seems at first merely two-dimensional, so too this play seems at first primarily a spritely comedy about witty and not-so-witty people; the allusions to painting reinforce that first impression. But as one looks more closely at a painting and finds elements which raise questions (what *is* that naked woman doing at the Manet picnic?) or which suggest a more complex world, so too *Love's Labour's Lost* turns out to be less consistent in tone and meaning than it first seems.

While Brook's production indicated directions for staging and for interpretation, its influence may also have extended to the change so evident in critical discussions of *Love's Labour's Lost*, particularly Anne Barton's 1953 essay. Barton's sense of the play echoes Brook's description of his inspiration: she mentions the 'haunting and beautiful kingdom' (Barton, p. 411) while he speaks of 'an autumn springtime' (Brook, *The Shifting Point*, p. 111); she describes Marcade's entrance 'unremarked by any of the other characters, materializing silently from those shadows which now lie deep along the landscape of the royal park' (p. 424), while Brook carefully staged the fight between Armado and Costard so that everyone onstage – and, one assumes, in the audience – would focus on the downstage action and thus not see Marcade until he walked quietly over the central mound. Just as Brook used the elegant world of Watteau as a visual equivalent to the artifice of the language and then the appearance of Marcade as a reminder that death can invade that lovely and protected world, so Anne Barton, and after her a number of other critics, make us see the language of the play not as decorative for its own sake, but decorative because the characters are defending themselves against time and death. Indeed, as she notes, the opening lines of the play express 'that peculiarly Renaissance relationship of the idea of Fame with that of Time and Death' (Barton, p. 412).

The lasting importance of Brook's production, Hunt's production, and Anne Barton's essay, coming as they did within a few years of each other, is that directors and critics gained a new perspective on the play from them, one which not merely recognised the delight and beauty of the final songs, but saw them as integral to the play. William C. Carroll's final chapter, 'Hiems and Ver', in the best book-length study of the play available, perceptively notes the complexity of those songs, the 'word of fear' in Spring, the 'merry note' of Winter, and argues: 'We choose, not one season over the other, but both. There is no other possibility' (p. 224). Barry Jackson's comments on the production he had helped to create by bringing Peter Brook to Stratford also stress, as Carroll does, the sense of conflicting but inseparable moods:

> The combination of Shakespeare's lines and the fragile Watteauesque atmosphere, therefore, seemed to me to be entirely right – the frail comedy of youth thus enwrapped in a delicate beauty remaining for me one of my unforgettable memories of the stage. (Barry Jackson, p. 80)

[55]

CHAPTER IV

'A pleasant conceited comedie': BBC Television, 1984

Given the influence, perhaps even the mystique, of Brook's production, it is not strange that almost forty years later Elijah Moshinsky, directing *Love's Labour's Lost* for the BBC series, would speak of the play in terms of 'the atmosphere of Marivaux – which is rather delicious and yet full of formalised rules between men and women, sense against sensibility; there's a distinction between enlightenment and feeling', and then add:

> I think the atmosphere of Watteau's paintings suits this enormously well and gives it a lightness of touch. And also it abstracts it; we don't want anything too realistic because the whole thing is a kind of mathematical equation – four men for four women – and the play is testing certain propositions about love. (Fenwick, p. 18)

By the time the six-year project of filming all of Shakespeare's plays for television was drawing to a close with, perhaps predictably, *Love's Labour's Lost* one of the last to be filmed and screened, the practice of using specific painters and even specific paintings to create the world of the plays was a well-established practice for the series. While the design of earlier productions had at moments created a 'realistic approach' (as in the 1979 *As You Like It* filmed at Glamis Castle) or somewhat generic 'period' approaches, the productions of the last four seasons often adopted a particular painter for the dominant visual signals. Jonathan Miller, who took over as producer from Cedric Messina, explains:

> you have an awkward situation, always, with the television when you're taking an art form which was not intended for that medium. One has to

understand that Shakespeare wrote for an unfurnished, unscenic stage without naturalistic representation of any sort. People didn't even wear colorful costumes. They simply wore modern costume, the costume of the sixteenth century, with perhaps some item which represented the past. Even in doing the Roman plays, it seems very unlikely that people wore archaeologically correct Roman costumes. Therefore I think it's very unwise to try and represent on the television screen something which Shakespeare did not have in his mind's eye when he wrote those lines. You have to find some counterpart of the unfurnished stage that Shakespeare wrote for without, in fact, necessarily reproducing a version of the Globe theatre. Because there's no way in which you can do that. You can't put one stage inside another, but you have to find some visual counterpart of that. (Hallinan, pp. 134-5)

Whether or not one agrees with Miller's generalisations, there is no doubt that his notion of using a 'visual counterpart' drawn from famous painters influenced directors for the last four years of the series. Painters more or less contemporary with Shakespeare inspired both set and costume design: Veronese for *Antony and Cleopatra*, Vermeer for *The Taming of the Shrew* (Miller comments that if one wants domestic interiors at this period one has to go to Dutch painting), Titian and Canaletto for *The Merchant of Venice*.

One of the earliest successes with this approach was Moshinsky's *All's Well that Ends Well* (filmed July 1980, screened 1981), with its echoes of Vermeer, Rembrandt and Hals, a production widely praised for its subtlety as well as its design. All in all, Moshinsky would direct five plays for the BBC series, and with the exception of *A Midsummer Night's Dream* (1981), he seems to have specialised in the less familiar plays – *All's Well*, *Cymbeline* (1982), *Coriolanus* (1983), and finally *Love's Labour's Lost* in 1984 (first screened in 1985). In most of these productions he drew on painters for set and design as well as lighting concepts: Rembrandt's 'Danaë's Bower' and 'Danaë in the Pool' as well as some Rubensesque trees and frescoes for *A Midsummer Night's Dream*, and Rembrandt's portrait of Agatha Bass as inspiration for Imogen's costume in *Cymbeline*. Thus, though the use of Watteau by Moshinsky and his designer, Barbara Gosnold, involved a painter from a period considerably later than that of *Love's Labour's Lost* (while earlier statements from both Cedric Messina and Jonathan Miller had suggested that all productions in the series would be set in a period earlier than or contemporary with Shakespeare's), the only real difference is the move from Dutch to French paintings.

Moreover, as Gordon P. Jones makes clear in his analysis of the five Moshinsky productions, Moshinsky's basic approach was similar in each case. While creating a striking visual style for the play, he further unified or, as Jones would see it, simplified each play by cutting it, eliminating passages of verbal quibbling (particularly with characters such as Lavatch in *All's Well* or Menenius in *Coriolanus*), reducing asides, and, in some cases, rearranging scenes, often by shifting location within a particular scene. Thus, while the text of *Love's Labour's Lost* has nine separate scenes, there are eighteen in the television production (cf. Willis, p. 84). Moshinsky even added a scene after the first encounter of the men and the women. The text takes us from Boyet's report of the King's feelings (end of II.i) to Armado and Moth (beginning of III.i), but Moshinsky incorporated a scene of Berowne sitting in the library, trying to study, but clearly thinking about Rosaline. We hear Berowne in a voice-over speaking the first six lines of the sonnet he sends to Rosaline; meanwhile a crystal ball on a pendulum swings back and forth across the desk, expressing his own inner conflict. On the fifth line, 'Study his bias leaves', he reaches out and stops the pendulum, and his face clearly shows that he is going to concentrate on Rosaline rather than on the books in front of him.

Another major change involves the rearrangement of I.i and I.ii. In the text Armado is mentioned in the middle of I.i after the four men have signed the oath, and then Dull arrives, with Costard in tow and Armado's letter in hand. But in the BBC production, the King's description of Armado, 'One who the music of his own vain tongue / Doth ravish like enchanting harmony' (I.i.165-6) is accompanied by Spanish-sounding guitar music. The library scene dissolves to Armado's lodging for the first part of I.ii, with Moth (John Kane) darning one of Armado's socks and Armado (David Warner) drooping against Moth's shoulder. The musical imagery of the King's words appears literally in the setting for Armado's room: a guitar lies in a chair, other musical instruments appear in the background, and when Armado orders Moth to sing, he picks up a bassoon and starts to play it himself, evoking a somewhat startled look from Moth. Shakespeare's scene continues with the entrance of Dull, Costard, and Jaquenetta, but at this point Moshinsky returns to the library for the second half of I.i and the reading of Armado's letter. At the end of I.i the King orders Costard delivered to Don Armado and the production picks up the second half of I.ii, showing Armado first in bed, but hastily leaping out when he hears not only that Costard is there but also that Jaquenetta is present. So Moshinsky cuts both I.i and I.ii in half and splices them together.

This breaking up of the text into shorter scenes is similar to the insertion of the little scene of Berowne 'thinking' since in both cases Moshinsky uses television's ability (which is also true of film) to tell a story quickly by *showing* the viewer something which the stage production may either allude to or describe. Thus the scene of Berowne fills in a kind of narrative gap, a gap which seems not to bother theatre audiences; when Berowne turns up in III.i with a letter for Rosaline, the audience assumes his 'offstage' activity of writing, an activity already signalled by the evident interest he has shown in Rosaline. Moshinsky's cutting from the description of Armado to the man himself, and then back to the scene in which the lords talk about him also represents story-telling on a very basic level, since he thus identifies for the audience a character who is not directly named on stage until V.i. But the scene-shifts also change the pace, perhaps bowing to television writing's fondness for shorter scenes, and thus break up the first two scenes so that they become four scenes. Moshinsky changes not merely the narrative pace but the visual pace as well, moving from the cool, off-white, high-windowed look of the library to the reds, browns, and over-stuffed appearance of Armado's room.

Not only does Moshinsky re-order the first two scenes, but he also cuts deeply Armado's and Moth's discussions of love, both in I.ii and again in III.i. Admittedly these scenes are often trimmed in stage productions – and one wonders whether the trimming is because the lines seem obscure or because they place a relatively heavy burden on the young actor playing Moth. Of all roles for children in Shakespeare's plays, Moth is perhaps the most complicated in terms of language, since his scenes involve continual punning and extended developed metaphors. In fact, only in 1936 did Tyrone Guthrie cast a boy, Gordon Miller, in the role so obviously meant for a boy-actor; before that time, grown-up (though small) actresses and actors had taken the part. Brook's production featured David O'Brien, a fifteen-year-old who also played (with much less success) Ariel the same season, and recent productions have swung back and forth between petite actresses (such as Amanda Root, Stratford-upon-Avon, 1984) and boys (such as Jo James, Stratford-upon-Avon, 1978). Given the number of times that characters mention Moth's diminutive size and his youth, it is somewhat startling that Moshinsky cast an adult actor John Kane (best known for his Puck in Brook's 1970 *A Midsummer Night's Dream*) in the role – and even more startling to find that with an actor who could certainly handle all the lines, so many of them were cut. Perhaps, as Susan Willis suggests (*The BBC Shakespeare Plays*, p. 156), the decision came from Moshinsky's preference for using actors with whom he had worked before, even though the series's literary advisor, John Wilders, protested against using an adult; perhaps Moshinsky hoped that the references to 'boy' would seem 'another of Armado's verbal eccentricities' (*The BBC Shakespeare Plays*, p. 162). Whatever the reasons for the choice, the result is a dampening of the comic tension generated in Shakespeare's text where a young boy consistently one-ups an older man in witty repartee.

The smoothing-out and editing of the Armado/Moth scenes is just one aspect of Moshinsky's 'partial' vision of the world of the play, as Gordon Jones has argued; furthermore, 'The distinctive if uncultivated voices of Armado, Moth, Holofernes, Costard, Dull, and Jaquenetta are all muffled by extensive cutting. The spontaneous, the natural, the vulgar, and the absurd are cut away to maintain the stylistic elegance that is the keynote of Moshinsky's adaptation of *Love's Labour's Lost*' (Jones, p. 198). His argument gains support from the visual treatment of these characters, since many of them look quite similar to the more 'upper-class' characters. Granted, Costard wears a brown burlap coat rather than the fine broadcloth of the courtiers-as-scholars or the satin of their first and last appearances, but Dull's wig is just as elegant as Boyet's. Sir Nathaniel and Holofernes appear also in enormous and fashionable wigs, and in coats resembling those of the scholars. Moshinsky does quietly suggest Armado's poverty with the opening shot of Moth darning a sock, but the predominant look for Armado is brocade, both in private (a gorgeous bathrobe which he hastily flings over his nightgown) and in public (his heavily embroidered waistcoat for V.i and an elaborately woven costume for Hector). Jaquenetta, in her early scenes, wears a relatively plain dark dress, but she shows less bosom than do the French ladies, and her hair is neatly pulled back and up, so there is nothing overtly sexual in her appearance.

The production's design stresses the formality of the world in which the characters live, particularly the opening scene in the King's library. The room is elegant, painted in off-white, with high rounded windows providing both light and a patterned background. All four of the men wear powdered wigs and rich velvet coats and knee-breeches; the King is in warm beige, Longaville in deep salmon, Dumaine in deep gold and Berowne in blue–grey. When we meet the women, their costumes will instantly reveal the pairing, with each woman dressed in a lighter shade of the one worn by the man who will fall in love with her. The props also stress formality, especially the model of a neoclassical building to which the camera pans while the King says 'Navarre shall be the wonder of the world' (I.i.12) as if to show just how balanced, clean, and elegant the 'little academe' will be. The use of the library may go back to Brook, but whereas the stage can easily present a stylised version of a library, the television camera needs things to look at. This library is crowded with objects, from the gold clock (a reminder of 'cormorant devouring Time'?) which appears behind the King's right shoulder as he begins the play, to the book-lined shelves, to the huge table, covered with crimson, about which they stand to sign their oaths, to the four copies of the oath (stage productions normally have just one) carefully arranged around the table.

The advantage of starting with such a formal place and with costumes of such artificiality (particularly, for a twentieth-century audience, the wigs) is that any slight change of style thereafter can register with much more force. In the opening scene, the introduction of Berowne gains power because of such small variations. His blue–grey costume is taken from a range of colours quite different from the three warmer shades of the other men; he does not stand with Dumaine and Longaville, flanking the King, but is separate; and unlike the others, he does not stand up straight, but *leans* against a bookshelf. Since Berowne will be the one to challenge the king's plan and to talk frankly of the needs of the flesh – 'O, these are barren tasks, too hard to keep, / Not to see ladies, study, fast, not sleep' (I.i.47-8) – it is significant that the camera first picks him up as the King mentions 'the huge army of the world's desires' (I.i.10), the kind of visual/verbal linking which Moshinsky exploits throughout the play. Similarly, the casual stance of Berowne, particularly in contrast with the other men, points to the conflict between a world of unnatural vows and a world of natural feelings.

The introduction of the Princess and her women again juxtaposes formality and a more natural style, and does so even more quickly. No sooner do the women in their elegant gowns come into view than the Princess sits down on a broad stone terrace – no chairs are there, just the step itself. That movement, coming as it does with Boyet's flattery, 'Yourself, held precious in the world's esteem' (II.i.4), immediately undercuts Boyet's line and suggests that the Princess does not take herself as seriously as he does. Indeed, her first lines, 'Good Lord Boyet, my beauty, though but mean, / Needs not the painted flourish of your praise' (II.i.13-14) further emphasise her lack of pretension. In contrast, Boyet, invited to sit down beside the Princess to receive her instructions, first brushes off the step with his handkerchief while the Princess flashes an ironic glance at Rosaline.

These two settings, the library and the park, echoing perhaps Brook's two main settings, alternate throughout the play, with a third set, Armado's room, used for three short scenes (the two parts of I.ii and then the first half of III.i). Although Armado's room seems claustrophobic and cluttered in contrast with the openness of the library and the park–terrace, the sense of formal design still comes through, particularly in the arrangement of actors on the screen. For their opening conversation Moth and Armado sit back to back, looking very much as if they are posing for a portrait, 'servant and master'. In the second half of that scene, Jaquenetta and Armado stand in front of a small window, so that they are silhouetted against it for their monosyllabic conversation. At the end of I.ii, Armado stands by the door of his room, almost not moving, as he soliloquises about the effects of love on him. Again the effect is of a portrait – the Spaniard in love.

Once Moshinsky creates these three different places and three different 'looks', he starts to change them subtly. When he returns to the second part of I.ii, the four men are now in navy-blue jackets and breeches, the only decorative touch their white cravats; the change, both in time and in mood, from the opening sequence is clear. The removal of the wigs further stresses that change, as if the men are becoming more natural (Fenwick, p. 20), although if one believes Berowne's complaints, the academic life is actually less natural than the court life. Perhaps the ironic point, both of play and television production, is that the decision to forsake the 'world's desires' is actually the impetus for confronting those desires more directly.

Indeed, throughout the production, Moshinsky uses not just costume but also hair-styles to signal changes between formality and relaxation. When Holofernes and Sir Nathaniel first appear, watching the hunt from the library, they are fully bewigged. Halfway through IV.ii, just before Jaquenetta and Costard come in with the letter, Moshinsky shifts from the library to a place marked in the BBC text as 'Arches' (another part of the park, with stone arches in the background). Holofernes is still wearing his wig, but Nathaniel sits and reads, with his wig hanging on the chair behind him, and a comfortable straw hat on his head. Thus, when Jaquenetta and Costard come in they naturally find themselves more at ease with Nathaniel. And, at the end of the scene, when Holofernes invites Nathaniel to dinner (Dull has somehow vanished with the scene change), it is only appropriate that Nathaniel should put his wig back on, because they are about to go into society. Given the necessity of re-wigging before dining, it is slightly surprising to find Holofernes without his wig when we see him finishing dinner (V.i) – and even more surprising to find that the dinner table is set in the library. But certainly the arrival of Armado sends Holofernes back to the more formal look as he puts his wig on to greet the Spanish guest. The lack of consistency in wig-wearing for both Holofernes and Nathaniel could suggest merely lapses on the part of the continuity editor since, according to Susan Willis, Moshinsky was 'excited by the set and by the wealth of props' and 'quickly invented business to use them' (*The BBC Shakespeare Plays*, p. 162). Yet the effect of watching both Nathaniel and Holofernes put their wigs back on is that we see each man constructing his social façade; for a few minutes he can be 'private', but then dresses himself for the more public moments.

Moshinsky also uses conventions of dress and hair-style to show us different views of the women. When the women appear at the beginning of V.ii (see Figure IV), they are arranged picturesquely on the terrace, the Princess seated in the centre, Rosaline reclining on one side, Katharine on the other (so that they can face each other, still recumbent, for the 'quarrel' at the beginning of the scene), Maria behind Katharine and the Princess. When the Muscovites enter, Moshinsky moves to an atmospheric, but non-naturalistic change of scene and costume; the scene dissolves into a shot of candles, casting shadowy light everywhere, and the women have suddenly acquired black lacy veils so that they can fool the Muscovites. After the men leave, Moshinsky inserts a change of place (the BBC text gives a new setting, 'Green Bank', for the lines beginning with 'Twenty adieus, my frozen Muscovites' [V.ii. 265]) and of time. The text implies a 'girl-talk' scene, with the women swapping notes about what the men said to them, and the verbal relaxation is echoed by the visual changes: Maria is in her underclothes having her corset laced up; both the Princess and Rosaline have their hair down; none of the women wear the necklace/ruffs seen earlier; Rosaline's dress is less tightly fitted and the Princess appears in a chemise top rather than the low-cut satin-with-brocade bodice of the first scene. The giggling between lines and the imitation of the over-dramatic lines of the men (lines which the audience has not heard) add to the visual impression of seeing the women less formally attired than at any other point in the play. Undressed implies unguarded, except for the always fully dressed Boyet, whose presence thus emphasises the informality of this particular conversation. It is as if the figures in a Watteau canvas have become so excited by the action of the previous scene that they have to move from their poses.

While most of the action of the production is essentially that of verbal fencing, a kind of witty duelling suitable for the elegance of the costumes and the setting, there are occasional moments when physical action reveals the emotional struggle within characters – and most of these moments belong to Berowne. Not only does Berowne's costume set him apart, but Mike Gwilym's relaxed stance and informality of movement constantly remind us that Berowne was reluctant to adopt the oath and in some sense is always fighting against it. Thus when the King reads Armado's letter in I.i, Moshinsky cuts to reaction shots of Berowne laughing or trying to stifle his laughter. When Dumaine, Longaville, and Berowne return in II.i to ask Boyet about the names of the ladies, the text suggests similar entrances for Dumaine and Longaville, since Dumaine begins with 'Sir, I pray you, a word' (II.i. 193) and Longaville with 'I beseech you a word' (196); Moshinsky underlines the parallel by having each enter screen left and then quickly back out. Berowne's first line is clearly less polite and more direct, 'What's her name in the cap?' (II.i. 208). The difference becomes visual as well, since he enters from screen right and crosses in front of Boyet, physically invading his space. Left alone in the library, at the end of III.i, Berowne paces restlessly; when he speaks of 'Dan Cupid', he imitates for a second the traditional pose of the flying Cupid, one foot up, the hands aiming an arrow. Even objects seem to take on life around Berowne – the swinging crystal ball, or the nude statue in the library to whom he gives an accusing look when he complains angrily that he loves a *woman*! As his anger mounts, he becomes like the objects around him – swinging his hand in pendulum gestures to illustrate the 'German clock' and ending up between two large astronomical instruments with his arms out, almost 'crucified' for his self-pitying complaint, 'Well, I will love, write, sigh, pray, sue, groan, / Some men must love my lady, and some' – followed by a pause which implies 'this is just my luck' – 'Joan' (III.i.199-200).

In IV.iii, Berowne mounts to the top of a circular staircase (the library substitute for a tree) and looks down on the other men as the King asks 'What will Berowne say?' (IV.iii.142). He drops a book to attract their attention, remaining, feet up on the balustrade, as he chastises them, the carelessness of the pose echoing the condescension in his parent-like question, 'Where lies thy grief?' (IV.iii.168). But the most startling moment in the scene comes when he starts to tear up the letter which Jaquenetta and Costard have brought, only to have it snatched from him by Dumaine and Longaville. Without thinking, he attacks Costard, Jaquenetta defends Costard by jumping on Berowne, and Dumaine tries to pull her off. The four of them end in a heap on the floor – Costard at the bottom – and the visual image of 'four fools' is striking, but even more so the undignified scuffling which has so unexpectedly preceded that tableau. The other men are infected by this behaviour, with Longaville pulling off his shoe as he taunts Berowne about Rosaline. In fact, Dumaine's comment, 'Then, as she goes, what upward lies/The street should see as she walked overhead' (IV.iii.276-7), almost starts another fight. But the King stops them verbally, and equilibrium, symbolised by the model of the King's academe, returns. When Berowne finds 'some authority how to proceed' (IV.iii.283) he does so as a university lecturer talking to three seated students, with a table and the model of the academe behind him; only his stance, one foot on a chair, reminds us that he is still less formal than the others.

One wonders whether the informality of Gwilym's Berowne owed anything to the fact that in 1973 Gwilym had played Costard in the RSC production directed by David Jones with Ian Richardson as Berowne. Gwilym comments on his difference from Richardson – and the connections he found between himself and Berowne:

I'd played Costard with Ian Richardson playing Berowne, and he was really fabulous in the part. We did it for a long time and I remembered absolutely everything he did, so a lot of the rehearsal for me was trying to put that behind me. On those terms I can't compete with him – he's like a machine-gun, which is so wonderful for Berowne. His brain is so razor-sharp he can go like billyo and his brain is still ahead of his mouth – and with Berowne it's easy for it to be the other way round! But it's a matter of being realistic about what you do that is different from what other actors do – it's a weaning process. My sort of humour is quite different from Ian's. My humour is malicious – it's a terrible admission to make, but it is. If I get a laugh it's usually at somebody's expense and that's a quality Berowne has. (Fenwick, p.23)

Gwilym's more relaxed manner makes his approach to Berowne's lines less a function of intellect (as with Richardson) and more a matter of his detached, ironic view of the world. The contrast between an alertly cynical Berowne and a casually ironic one revealed itself in the striking differences between the two actors. Richardson's Berowne was not just mentally quick but also physically so. He always seemed to enter the stage at a run, the fast pace of body revealing the fast pace of his mind. And occasionally his body would betray him, as in the hilarious moment during the overhearing scene when Dumaine, instead of merely reading his sonnet, burst into song, and Berowne lost his grip, almost fell out of the tree, and swung back and forth until he was hidden again. A few minutes later when the King handed over Berowne's own sonnet, Richardson's Berowne was so flustered that he frantically tore it to pieces, not realising how his action has thus betrayed him. Except for the 'fight' in the library, Gwilym's Berowne seemed much more casual, someone who lounged rather than ran. Yet at crucial moments, such as the long speech in IV.iii when Berowne has to 'justify' the broken oaths, Richardson and Gwilym were remarkably similar. Richardson just stood in one place, working through the argument with intellectual passion. Richard David's comment, 'It flowed and it glowed but remained a prize oration' (*Shakespeare in the Theatre*, p.132) would apply just as well to Gwilym's lecture. Gwilym himself sees Berowne as a character who 'never changes right through to the end of play', with the big speech not a turning-point, but a 'con'. He adds: 'If it was a true turning-point there'd be no reason for the men to go to the women disguised as Russians! That's just a continuation of the same old game – you don't have to speak the truth, you put on a mask and then you can say anything' (p. 22).

While Gwilym's casting and approach to the role seem consonant with his past experience not just with *Love's Labour's Lost*, but in other major Shakespearean roles (Edgar, Troilus, Theseus/ Oberon at the RSC, plus Aufidius in *Coriolanus* and the title role in *Pericles* for the BBC series), the casting of Maureen Lipman as the Princess of France is something no one could have predicted.

Known primarily as a TV comedienne (and now making a fine living with her Beatie character for British Telecom commercials), Lipman seemed surprised that she was even offered the role (Willis, p. 71). Her comic ability, muted into ironic pauses, inflections, and glances, is particularly evident in her first scene, as she crisply and effectively cuts off Boyet's praises, and then sends him out with a letter; her slight lilt when she describes her group as 'humble-visag'd suitors' (II.i.34) implies very gently that she is not at all used to such a role. When the King comes in, the speed of her replies to his polite greetings implicitly reminds him that words are much less polite than instant accommodation would be. Her tone is slightly tart, and her look, emphasised by her longish face with hair pulled tightly back, is that of the current Princess Royal, another no-nonsense royal lady. The King counters her unspoken criticism by suggesting he will come to a decision as soon as possible. His verbal underlining of 'suddenly' in 'Madam, I will, if suddenly I may' (II.i.110) manages to imply with some condescension that important state matters sometimes take longer than one would wish. Lipman's Princess will not let even this mild rebuke pass unnoticed, so she fires back, 'You will the sooner that I were away' (II.i.111), thus making the point that if he wants her to leave, he should not delay his decision. All of this skirmishing remains polite, and the Princess later controls her anger when the King implies that her father's demands were unreasonable and even perhaps contrary to the facts. But as the King and his men leave, we hear her exhaled breath of irritation.

The hostility evident between Navarre and the Princess thus leads to her mixture of disbelief and amusement when Boyet, after the King's departure, speaks of the King's 'eye, peeping thorough desire' (II.i.234). But her laughter turns to listening, her attentiveness revealed by the way her teacup remains in mid-air while Boyet continues his persuasion. At first the audience's reaction and that of the Princess are the same – namely that Boyet is making this up, since nothing in the preceding scene suggested such feelings from the King. But the more the Princess listens, the more she seems to accept at least the possibility of the king's love. Moshinsky's comment makes the point explicit:

> The Princess doesn't fall in love, I don't think, in the first scene between her and the King. Boyet, her courtier, reports to her that the King has fallen in love with her – then she gets the idea and looks at him from a distance and is almost amused by the fact that this man had fallen in

love with her. I don't think it's an inevitable love story between the Princess and the King at all. I think Boyet plays the role of Cupid, of Pandarus. He makes it happen by gossiping. (Fenwick, p. 8)

Such a reading, which is essentially anti-romantic, may well have influenced his casting choice of Maureen Lipman – or it may have developed from the personality of the actress. The qualities she projects are those of composure, maturity, and irony, all expressed through a slightly school-marmish tone, rather than those of a woman who immediately falls for the King. Thus both Moshinsky's view and Lipman's portrayal make utterly plausible the Princess's reaction to the King's proposal at the end of the play when she explains that the women 'met your [i.e. the men's] loves / In their own fashion, like a merriment' (V.ii.776). She has not been fooled into falling in love, and she remains somewhat sceptical at the end of the play.

The anti-romantic approach also colours, somewhat literally, Moshinsky's view that Berowne and Rosaline are 'rather ill-matched', and hence his choice to make Berowne 'enormously blond' in contrast to the dark Rosaline specified by the text (Fenwick, p. 9). Similarly, the antagonism between Berowne and Rosaline, while more sexually charged than that between the King and the Princess, seems very much a struggle for power. Their first encounter, while the King reads the letter from France, is a series of one-upmanship ploys, with only Berowne's line 'And send you many lovers' (II.i.125) implying a particular interest. Moshinsky cuts their second series of one-liners, thus leaving out Berowne's 'Lady, I will commend you to mine own heart' (II.i.179), a much more sincere-sounding line than his previous opening, 'Did not I dance with you in Brabant once?' (II.i.113). The couple do not appear together again until the final scene, and when we see them separately, both text and production emphasise their unwilling interest in the other, an interest particularly evident in Berowne's soliloquy (III.i) as he paces in irritation around the library. Rosaline's speech about wanting to 'torture' Berowne (V.ii. 60-7) is filmed in close-up, almost as if Rosaline is thinking to herself and revealing thoughts she may not have been aware of earlier. His request at the end, 'Impose some service on me for thy love' (V.ii.832) implies that he realises he will have to do *something* to show her he is serious, but Gwilym's tone also conveys the sense, 'what a waste of time'. When Rosaline requires him 'To enforce the pained impotent to smile' (V.ii.846), Berowne's objection is both verbal – 'To move wild laughter in the throat of death? / It cannot be; it is impossible' (V.ii.847-8) – and physical – he turns away from Rosaline and then turns back. In contrast, Rosaline remains utterly still and, it seems, emotionally unmoved. Her accusation that his wit 'is begot of that loose grace / Which shallow laughing hearers give to fools' (V.ii.851-2) stresses the word 'fools', reminding both him and us of the way she had earlier asked ironically, 'All the fool mine?' (V.ii.384). Not until his acceptance of her terms does he smile at her – and receive a smile in return.

The lack of romantic attachment between the characters in the production is not surprising, given Moshinsky's sense of 'mis-match' for the two central couples. He argues that the play

> is a kind of situation comedy using 'love' to explore comedy and reality and what real feelings are. The central concern is the discovery of what true feelings are and what comedy is and whether if you have a comic frame of mind you *can* experience reality. Berowne, as Rosaline says, is a man 'replete with mocks' and he cannot experience reality. Rosaline herself, as Katharine says, has 'a merry, nimble, stirring spirit' and doesn't feel deeply. (Fenwick, pp. 24-5)

In one sense, Moshinsky's comment explains the distance from romantic feelings that his production presents. Since he believes Rosaline's characterisation of Berowne and Katharine's of Rosaline, he then assumes that their feelings are not very deep, that they are 'in love with the idea of love' (Fenwick, p. 24) rather than with each other. Against such a commentary, one might point to the enormous resistance Berowne offers to the idea of being in love, a resistance so forceful that he seems to 'protest too much', and thus must be in love. One corollary of Moshinsky's view is that the separation of the men and women at the end of the play may well be entirely appropriate, rather than 'love's labour's lost'.

Moshinsky's concern with 'true feelings' and 'reality' might have led him to focus on the love relationships and the way in which those change from mockery to something deeper. Instead, those concerns push him towards what might be called the 'meta-theatrical' approach, in which one thinks of a play as concerned with its own theatricality. Thus the Pageant of the Nine Worthies and the entrance of Marcade are, in Moshinsky's view, an 'astonishing sleight of hand about reality and the reflection of experiencing reality' (Fenwick, p. 25); the offstage audience watching the courtiers watch the Pageant forgets that everything is unreal and thus experiences a shock of 'reality' similar to that experienced by the Princess, her ladies, and the King's court. Moshinsky's description immediately reminds one of Puck's epilogue to *A Midsummer Night's Dream*, a play Moshinsky had directed for the BBC series three years earlier (May 1981); Moshinsky's assertion that 'in the end you think the play [*Love's Labour's Lost*] is about the process of conning the audience, which is one of the feelings you also get at the end of *The Dream*' (Fenwick, p. 25) makes the connnection clear.

Moshinsky's emphasis on issues of artifice and reality, rather than on the romantic relationships of the men and women, creates a version of the Pageant of the Nine Worthies which is the high point of the production. Paradoxically, though he speaks frequently about the closing sequences of the play, from the Pageant on, in terms of artifice, it is also the part of the play in which true feelings, although not true romantic feelings, are most evident. Moshinsky returns from the exterior set – where the Muscovites tried to woo the women – to the library, now transformed into a little theatre with a red-draped stage at one end, servants holding candelabras, and rows of chairs for the watchers; already, he reminds the watching audience, the focus has shifted into an artificial world. Off-screen music announces each character, supplied perhaps by Moth (who has earlier been heard playing a violin) and by Armado (his bassoon is clearly recognisable), as well as the traditional knocks with a staff, supplied by Dull. The Pageant blends humour with pathos, especially when Sir Nathaniel, dressed in what seem to be orange satin pyjamas, starts his lines all over again only to be met with the audience's scornful 'Oh' and rhythmic clapping designed to shoo him offstage. Pompey appears from backstage, first chastises Nathaniel – 'A conqueror and afeard to speak! Run away for shame, Alisander' (V.ii.573-4) – and then, as Nathaniel bursts into tears, gently embraces him while explaining to the audience, 'alas! you see how 'tis – a little o'erparted' (V.ii.579). Comedy returns with Moth's Hercules, dressed in white satin, with a hand puppet for the snake: as he turns to leave, we see that he is on his knees, crawling upstage, and when he gets to the edge of the platform, he falls backstage. Holofernes' Judas, resplendent in a gold satin Greek tunic (as re-imagined by the eighteenth century), initially is able to control the audience in the tone that he clearly uses with unruly boys. When the insults continue, he consults with Dull (the book-keeper) and then decides to leave. But he cannot find the opening in the curtain and keeps trying to do so, while Boyet jeers, 'why dost thou stay?' Eventually, Moth comes to his rescue; the hand with the snake puppet on it appears through an opening and tries to wave him in the right direction. But Holofernes, in his confusion, does not see Moth's helping hand and scrambles off the front of the stage, an ominous fabric-tearing sound accompanying his undignified exit. In all of these comic 'bits', the discrepancy between the brave, even elegant, façade implied by the satin costumes and the collapse of each character reminds us of the human beings who are struggling to put on the show.

David Warner's Armado backs onto the stage, but his romanticised Hector is no more welcome than Holofernes' pompous Judas. The interruptions and perhaps the lavish rhetoric seem to bore Rosaline, who leans over and whispers to the Princess while Hector says 'when he breathed, he was a man' (V.ii.654-5) – and he gently rebukes the Princess with 'Sweet royalty, bestow on me the sense of hearing' (V.ii.656-7). Her embarrassment at being impolite is nothing compared to the embarrassment of Jaquenetta, whom Costard suddenly drags on stage, through the curtain, with the announcement 'Fellow Hector, she is gone. She is two months on her way' (V.ii.664-5). There is no time to figure out who the father is or why Costard should choose to reveal the news at this time, because the camera focuses our attention on Jaquenetta's tears and Armado's frantic attempt to remove his glove in order to slap Costard's face. Once again, as in the overhearing scene, the formal atmosphere breaks up; people rise from their chairs, others move the chairs out of the way, and the camera cuts quickly from one shot to another. Though Pompey takes off his multicoloured jacket and reveals his white shirt, Armado refuses to fight, and admits quietly 'I have no shirt. I go woolward for penance' (V.ii.701-2). He smiles shyly, almost inviting the audience to enjoy the joke – as indeed they do, with laughter rippling through the court and growing.

In many stage productions this section of text builds to elaborate physical comedy, as with the antics of Costard in Brook's production or the frenetic game of 'keep-away' played with Jaquenetta's dishclout in Barton's 1978 production (cf. Chapter VI). But that kind of comedy takes stage space which is simply not available to the small television screen, and so Moshinsky's choice is to use Armado's laughter and the concomitant laughter from the court as the 'merriment' which a cut to Marcade interrupts. He stands on the stage, black suit and white cravat, and has to speak 'God save you, madam!' over the laughter. The Princess still does not realise what's wrong, 'Welcome, Marcade; / But that thou interruptest our merriment.' But then two shots, first on 'Dead, for my life', and then a close-up as Marcade says 'My tale is told' (V.ii.707-9, 712-13) show us her shock and pain. The room is suddenly silent: the Princess crosses in front of the others as if they are not even there and sits on the front of the stage beneath Marcade. The change of mood depends on this moment, and on the feeling that all the merriment, whether it is laughing at Armado or enjoying the courtship 'jokes', has suddenly ended. The range of feelings during the Pageant, and especially the focus on the embarrassment and even pain of Nathaniel, Holofernes, Jaquenetta and Armado, argues against the 'single-faceted, designer-driven uniformity' described by Gordon Jones (p. 198). Indeed, the very artificiality of the setting, including the satin costumes, becomes a transparent façade through which we see the real people. Armado's shy smile epitomises both his humanity and the possibilities of television; such an expression would be lost on stage.

The final moments of the production give us multiple choices for understanding the play. Two women sing the final song, one dressed in yellow (Spring), the other in grey (Winter), and the camera offers us dissolving shots of the four courtly couples, with close-ups of *each* character to emphasise their isolation. The combination of words and pictures seems to predict either infidelity (we see the King on 'Mocks married men' and the Princess on 'Cuckoo') or a chilly relationship ('When icicles hang by the wall' takes us to Dumaine and Katharine, 'Dick the shepherd' to Longaville, 'Tom bears logs' to Maria, and 'milk comes frozen home in pail' first to Rosaline and then to Berowne). Only Armado (now in a long red gown) and Jaquenetta are together, leaning against the stage, his arm around her. The last image on the screen is of these two, and we hear Armado say 'The words of Mercury are harsh after the songs of Apollo' and then, in voice-over, 'You that way; we this way.' The singing continues during the credits, and at the end the two singers overlap, so that we hear 'Cuckoo, cuckoo' and 'Greasy Joan doth keel the pot' simultaneously. Visually the resolution is one of stasis, and, except for Armado and Jaquenetta, a kind of communal isolation, but aurally the production insists that Spring and Winter exist in harmony together.

Is such harmony really possible? Moshinsky creates it by placing the entire production in a world that is always artificial and formal, a world without trees or bushes. The overhearing scene, as I have mentioned, gives Berowne the vantage point of a library staircase rather than a tree, and the King emerges from behind a bookcase, holding a book, to confront Longaville and Dumaine with the lines 'I have been closely shrouded in this book / And marked you both, and for you both did look', since he clearly cannot say 'I have been closely shrouded in this bush, / And mark'd you both, and for you both did blush' (IV.iii.134-5). The 'rustics' seem less rustic, given the similarity of their appearance to the courtiers, especially when Holofernes, Nathaniel and Dull all wear their elaborate wigs. So the distance between art and nature is never far in this production, since the artificial so completely dominates.

Perhaps any production which opts for the elegance of the painterly tradition and so increases the audience's sense of artifice – in the play's language and in its setting – will inevitably raise the question of sincerity or seriousness for the major characters. The choice of the eighteenth-century setting particularly invites such questions, as the elegant costumes of the characters imply, at least to a twentieth-century audience, public appearance and correct manners rather than spontaneous feeling. The opening action of the play is highly susceptible to an ironic reading, since the formality of the language and the absurdity of the vows invite satiric commentary. David Jones's 1973 Stratford-upon-Avon production similarly emphasised that view by opening the play with an almost balletic ritual of leaving the world. Musicians played a melancholy fanfare that turned into a funeral march; servants marched in solemnly, carrying an open wooden coffin; the King and his friends ceremoniously divested themselves of their cloaks, hats, and gloves, throwing those 'worldly' items into the coffin and then arraying themselves in long blue scholarly robes. The straight faces of the characters – even at the moment when Berowne, Dumaine, and Longaville applauded Navarre's pronouncement, 'Navarre shall be the wonder of the world' and the King himself spun around the stage to show off his new scholarly attire – were irresistibly funny. Richard David found this opening 'an initial blunder' (*Shakespeare in the Theatre*, p. 131) precisely because it implied that 'the vow to study is no more than a silly prank' (p. 129); 'if,' he argued, 'the beginning of the play is too shallow there is a real risk that the wonderful deepening of mood that ends it will go for little' (p. 130). Moshinsky avoids such overt comedy at the beginning of his production, although he does insist on the formality of the occasion. But such formality, including the detail that *four* copies

[73]

of the oath have been placed on the table waiting for the men to sign, implies that whatever thought has gone into the making of the vow is over, and we are witnessing only the last stage in the ceremony.

In that sense, the view of the young men is always an ironic one, created not only by Berowne's words but by the production itself. And the lack of any real feeling between the young men and the young women, inherent in Moshinsky's views of the play, also creates detachment from their world. Reviews of the production respond to that detachment, whether one looks to Frances Teague's feeling that 'the production was so serene and careful that one lost sight of Shakespeare's quicksilver comedy' (p. 313) or to Peter Kemp's comment that the final moment 'when natural zest should well up simply and strongly in the ballad-like songs of Spring and Winter, gets titivated into a pseudo-Mozartian sequence of self-conscious operatic trills and cadenza fanciness' (*Times Literary Supplement*, 18 January 1985). Moshinsky aims, I think, at giving us the play as satire, but also protects himself by making the world pretty and elegant: 'Ladies in panniered silks – old gold, greenish grey, dusty pink – arrange themselves, their fans and ruffed wrists into picturesque groupings against a background of amber haze or russet distances' (Kemp, *TLS*).

The question that arises is the extent to which Moshinsky's interpretation of the play comes from the fact that he was directing it for television rather than the stage. Many of the details discussed in this chapter have their equivalents in stage production. But because television lacks immediate audience response, productions of comedies create special problems. Comedy thrives on the audience's laughter, as any actor who has played Costard figuring out the monetary difference between 'remuneration' and 'gardon' (III.i. 164-7) can attest. And it is precisely that silent void, the moment when no laughter comes although the lines and the delivery may invite them, that television must confront – or, perhaps, the possibility of that void, since an individual viewer at home may laugh, or may not. We expect that the laughter will be shorter for the individual watching television since there is no reinforcement from a large theatre audience, and so the actor and director must adjust the timing. Or, as in the case of Moshinsky's production of *A Midsummer Night's Dream*, the text surrounding the play-within-the-play may be cut to avoid the interruptions/comments of the onstage audience. Those comments work on stage in part because they increase the difficulties for the performers of 'Pyramus and Thisbe'; they must cope not only with Quince's bouncy rhymes but an audience that gets more and more intrusive, an audience which can reduce Moonshine to tears or anger. But, as Gordon Jones suggests, 'in the absence of a live theatrical or studio audience responding to the cumulative absurdity of the play-within-the-play, it is very difficult to make the scene work effectively and build to a comic climax. Removing some of the interjections and playing the episode straighter than usual is one way of making the best of a bad job' (Jones, p. 196).

Similarly, in *Love's Labour's Lost*, Moshinsky eliminates much of the physical comedy Costard often creates, especially in the build-up to the fight with Armado. Instead of physical action, there is camera action, with quick cuts implying the court's sense of excitement and anticipation and much laughter on the soundtrack giving us their reaction. One might argue that their laughter pre-empts or replaces ours. If the downplaying of comic moments is inevitable in televised comedy – and other productions in the BBC series, notably Jonathan Miller's *The Taming of the Shrew*, imply that it is – one can still ask about Moshinsky's interpretation of the play itself. His comments that *Love's Labour's Lost* is 'about the process of comedy, and what is serious and what is real,' or that it is 'about the structures and devices of comedy' (Fenwick, p. 21) imply, as I've indicated above, a metatheatrical view of the play, as if the play is constantly analysing itself. While isolated lines in the play, particularly Berowne's objections to waiting a year and a day for the ladies to marry the lords, do remind us of the gap between the play world where time passes quickly and the real world where it does not, Moshinsky's statements about the play as being about comedy move him away from direct confrontation with the characters.

Even more at issue, however, is Moshinsky's view of how the audience should *feel*, and here his comments suggest two opposing views. On the one hand, he argues that 'Feelings aren't real – feelings are stated theoretically … . We don't go into the depths of his [the King's] character, like some other plays' (Fenwick, p. 21). But then he suggests that the play grows out of the tension between 'artificiality and reality' and that, 'at the end of the play, which is its greatest point, people break through into a new sense of reality and feeling' (Fenwick, p. 21). If Moshinsky wanted to create the sense of real feelings, television could certainly serve him well, since its close-ups give us, as Gary F. Waller strongly demonstrates, an intimate sense of people's feelings: '[Television's] most powerful image, at once metonymy and metaphor, is the human face. The television actor expresses himself not, as on the stage, in body movements, but in facial change' (p. 22). In a few moments, most notably the close-up of the Princess when she finally registers the death of her father, Moshinsky achieves that intimacy and we share the character's feelings. But for the most part, we watch people avoiding feeling, and the camera avoiding emotional revelation. Such a reading of *Love's Labour's Lost* has a certain validity, but less so in the latter half of the twentieth century, when major productions have shown just how much feeling the play might actually contain. Moreover, given the power of television to reveal what characters are feeling and thinking, this production seems to exploit the 'coolness' of the medium, but not its potential for emotional depth.

I Watteau's *Fête Vénitienne*. Courtesy of the National Galleries of Scotland.

II The final scene of Peter Brook's 1946 RSC production. Photo by Angus McBean.

III The would-be scholars meet the Princess (Glenda Jackson) and her court, II.i, in John Barton's 1965 production: Berowne (Charles Thomas) is at the far left while Rosaline (Janet Suzman) stares at him from the far right.

IV The Princess (Maureen Lipman, standing), with Katharine (Petra Markham, left), Rosaline (Jenny Agutter, centre) and Maria (Katy Behean, right) at her feet, scrutinises the King's 'favour' in V.i of the 1984 BBC production. Copyright BBC.

V The hunting scene, IV.i, in Michael Kahn's 1968 Stratford, Connecticut production. Diana van der Vlis (centre) as the Princess, flanked by Katharine (Marian Hailey), Forester (Carl Strano), Rosaline (Denise Huot) and Maria (Kathleen Dabney). Courtesy of The New York Public Library.

VI The Princess (Carmen Du Sautoy), with Maria (Sheridan Fitzgerald) to the left, Katharine (Avril Carson) arranging the Princess's hair, and Rosaline (Jane Lapotaire) to the right, II.i, in John Barton's 1978 RSC production.

VII Costard (Alan Hendrick), Dull (David Lyon) and Jaquenetta (Ruby Wax), front row, with Armado (Michael Hordern), Holofernes (Paul Brooke) and Nathaniel (David Suchet) behind them as they present the 'dialogue between the Owl and the Cuckoo' in John Barton's 1978 RSC production.

VIII Berowne (Michael Pennington) kneels to Rosaline (Jane Lapotaire) in the final moments of John Barton's 1978 RSC production.

CHAPTER V

'Some delightful ostentation': Stratford, Connecticut, 1968

Implicit in Moshinsky's use of designs, costumes, and stage pictures that were not merely elegant but also noticeably painterly is an attitude towards Shakespeare production that assumes a 'high art' status for the play. Brook's use of Watteau is similar, but his addition of *commedia dell'arte* figures (Holofernes and Nathaniel) and even a Victorian policeman (Dull) allows him to comment on that elegant world even while representing it. The tendency to show the world of *Love's Labour's Lost* as one of beauty and elegance may spring from various sources: 1) a sense that all Shakespeare plays belong to a tradition of high culture; 2) a desire to show that the male nobles in *this* play are merely playing at being scholars, just as Marie Antoinette and her court played at being shepherds and shepherdesses in a specially constructed palace; 3) a compensatory gesture to the audience, giving them a production that is as lovely to look at as the play is difficult to understand. Indeed, this last motive is particularly relevant to *Love's Labour's Lost*, since for many years literary critics have spoken about the play as a topical satire, poking fun at literary figures of the 1580s and 1590s.

One might surmise that it was this reputation as a topical piece which, in part, kept it from stage production for so long. After all, if the play is built on allusions to figures such as Thomas Nashe, John Florio, Gabriel Harvey, John Eliot, or even the better-known Sir Walter Ralegh and the Earl of Southampton, and if critics still argue about who is meant by what character, can an audience really follow the play without footnotes? (cf. David, Arden edition, pp. xxxii-xliii). Harley Granville-Barker called the play 'a satire, a comedy of affectations' (p. 1); Mark Van Doren labelled it 'Shakespeare's most topical piece' (p. 58); Richard David described the play as 'a battle in a private war between court factions' (p. xliii). Such insistence that the play is topical and satiric is difficult to shake off. Clearly the history of production shows other approaches, first to treat the play essentially as light entertainment and then to find ways of emphasising the darkness beneath that merriment. But no one seems to have tried presenting the play *as topical satire* until 1968 when Michael Kahn, at the American Shakespeare Festival in Stratford, Connecticut, directed a production which specifically took up that challenge, albeit with a modern twist. Instead of satirising Elizabethan literary affectation, Kahn focused on the affectations of 1960s popular culture. In so doing, he avoided treating the play as 'high art' but still found a way to stress what seemed to him central issues in the play while making those issues accessible to his audience and his actors.

Kahn's production opened in late June 1968. In February 1968 the Beatles, who had become not merely Britain's most famous group of pop singers, but objects of hysterical adulation from crowds of devoted fans, left their world of pop-star luxury to study in India with a guru. The study of transcendental meditation seemed to promise an escape from their own fame, although it inevitably raised sarcastic eyebrows all around the world, as the comments of William F. Buckley make clear:

> The doings of the Beatles are minutely recorded here in England and, as a matter of fact, elsewhere, inasmuch as it is true what one of the Beatle-gentlemen said a year or so ago, that they are more popular than Jesus Christ. It is a matter of considerable public interest that all four of the Beatles have gone off to a place called Rishikesh, in India, to commune with one Maharishi Mahesh Yogi. The gentleman comes from India, and the reigning chic stipulates that Mysterious India is where one goes to Have a Spiritual Experience. (Buckley, p. 23)

Thus no one watching Kahn's production could miss the fact that the three young men who promised to study with the King of Navarre were not French courtiers, but versions of the Beatles, especially since they were pursued by teenyboppers and camera-flashing reporters as they arrived for the first scene. Like the Beatles, they escaped the modern world to go to India/Navarre where the long haired and full-bearded King, accompanied by incense-bearers and a sitar player, wore a long white robe and, though noticeably younger than the Maharishi, obviously alluded to that cult figure. Boyet's costume and mannerisms recalled the flamboyant author of *Breakfast at Tiffany's* and *In Cold Blood*, Truman Capote, while the Princess of France and her women were characterised in one of the prompt books as 'Rich, Elegant, Swinging'. Most of the design choices focused on contemporary costumes, hairdos, and props, since Kahn left the stage itself relatively bare. The basic proscenium stage at the American Festival Theatre was covered with three hexagonally shaped platforms, one on top of the other, forming different acting areas with different levels; the back of the stage was hung with a large bamboo blind, dimly visible behind a curtain decorated with forest and floral motifs; wicker stools and potted plants were brought in when needed.

Kahn's choice to emphasise the contemporary analogues of the play grew in part out of his belief that the play 'was such a specific satire on Southampton's court and friends' that the Elizabethan audience would have realised the topicality (Kahn, Interview). The critic most prominent for Kahn seems to have been Harold Goddard, whose two-volume work, *The Meaning of Shakespeare*, was a familiar critical resource during the 1950s and 1960s in the United States. Perhaps the essentialist promise of the title, or the sweep of the work (a chapter on each of the plays), or the willingness to take an ironic look at plays such as *The Taming of the Shrew* ('The woman lords it over the man so long as she allows him to think he is lording it over her', p. 68, is a typical remark), helped to make Goddard's book popular in American academic institutions. At any rate, in a programme note (cited by Cooper, p. 140) Michael Kahn quotes Goddard on the idea of 'the intimate acquaintance of his audience with the affectations he was pillorying' (p. 48), an acquaintance he tried to re-create by using the affectations of the 1960s and by satirising contemporary figures such as the Beatles or Truman Capote. But Kahn also thought of a modern-dress production because he felt that his actors were uncomfortable with period costume and movement. Turning that seeming defect into an advantage, he decided to capitalise on the qualities he *did* see in his young actors, particularly their 'contemporary' style and energy (Kahn, Interview).

Presenting the play in a contemporary setting created a world that was simultaneously glamorous and yet easy to make fun of, a world in which the satire of 'trendiness of language and feeling' (Kahn, Interview) would be immediately recognisable. It was also a

[79]

world of high-spirited characters, reflecting in part the literary critics to whom Kahn was indebted (the souvenir programme commentary abounds in words such as 'exuberantly', 'animatedly', 'sheer vitality', 'lively energy', 'infectious delight', 'highest possible spirits'), and in part his sense that his young cast were 'very physical' rather than keenly intellectual. Thus the production's noisy pre-show, with cameras flashing and teenyboppers first trying to tear off the men's clothes and then being carried or dragged offstage by the guards, opened the play with a burst of energy. The next major entrance, that of the Princess and her ladies, was even more spectacular – on motor scooters! The Princess, wearing a silver lamé jumpsuit, drove in first, followed by Boyet and Rosaline and Katharine (on foot), and then Maria on another motor scooter – and at the end of their scene, they drove off again.

The Beatles dominated the play not just as emblematic figures (superstars retreating from the world) but also in terms of their anarchic spirit preserved on film in *A Hard Day's Night* (1964) and *Help!* (1965), films short on plot but rich in slapstick, chase scenes, and visual gags. Such a spirit influenced the production's treatment of IV.iii, the multiple overhearing scene, a scene which became progressively more exuberant in its treatment of the men's 'sonnets'. The entrance of the King became a ritual, for instead of simply reading aloud the sonnet he has written to the Princess, he waves in the sitar player, who is then followed by a servant carrying a mat and small pot of incense; only when his 'set' is ready does he recite his poem to the sitar's accompaniment. Berowne hides behind a potted plant; stepping up on to the large pot, and peering over the plant, he delivers his sarcastic comments. The King chooses a similar plant for *his* hiding place and similarly pops up like a jack-in-the-box. When Longaville enters, he grabs a handmike from downstage right and sings his sonnet to a rock-and-roll beat. When I saw the production I remember thinking that no one could understand a single word, but that the very absorption in 'performance' is exactly the point. Longaville cares more for his performance than for Maria. And Dumaine's performance, also with a hand-held microphone, is even more extravagant, according to the promptbook:

> Dumaine violently throws music on floor.
> Dumaine moves down centre, 'whips' mike cord.
> Dumaine puts his free hand inside open kaftan he is wearing and runs it sensuously over his body.

Dumaine's hand moves down inside costume to groin.
Dumaine drops to knee and slowly rises.

Meanwhile, as he comes to the last few lines of the sonnet, the arms of Berowne, the King, and Longaville become visible behind their potted plants, and they offer a finger-snapping rhythmic accompaniment (Cooper, and promptbook).

Although the women were less specifically modelled on contemporary figures, they too participated in the extravagance of the concept. Their motorised entrance is just the beginning of a series of stunning tableaux. When they reappear in IV.i (the beginning of the second act in Kahn's production), they have, of course, changed their clothes – what else would those nine pieces of luggage carried by three servants suggest? The Princess wears the sort of outfit one might reasonably see on safari, long trousers, khaki jacket, the relative plainness of the ensemble setting off her long blonde hair. But the other women are clearly in some fantasy version of 'hunting' clothes, with Katherine and Maria in leopard-skin mini-skirts, Katherine's knee-high boots trimmed with leopard and Maria's boots reaching to mid-thigh, while Rosaline wears a mid-calf skirt that seems to be made from a tiger skin (See Figure V). The beginning of the last scene shows them each attended by a personal hairdresser, who fusses over his 'client' with hairspray and comb and mirror. Kahn commented that he wanted to do something slightly different with the '900th scene of people making jokes' and so he used the sense of a 'pajama party' to create the intimacy of 'talking about the guys'. The obvious homosexuality of the hairdressers attracted much attention from reviewers, and Kahn conceded that he wouldn't make those jokes any more (Kahn, Interview). Kahn's stereotyping not only seems questionable in the last decade of the twentieth century, but may have seemed so to New York theatre audiences who, in April 1968, could have seen Matt Crowley's *The Boys in the Band*, presenting what Clive Barnes called 'by far the frankest treatment of homosexuality I have ever seen on the stage' (*New York Times*, 15 April 1968). The effect of the hairdressing scene, suggested Bernard Beckerman, was to make the women 'as addled as the men' with 'the same flighty, insubstantial quality possessed by the court of Navarre' (p. 380). If one reads the presentation of the women less pejoratively, they seem apt counterparts for the men, able to match them in swinging fashion and sophistication – and the drinking of champagne during the Pageant of the Nine Worthies was just what one would expect.

[81]

One may ask whether Kahn's updating of the Princess and her women sufficiently differentiated the men and the women. Kahn called the men 'smug and charming and unaware' (Interview), but the same might be said of the women in this production, raising the question of whether they are the appropriate people to make the men aware of their own superficiality. There seems to be a conflict between Kahn's idea that the women saw the men 'as terribly in need of a lesson in humanity' (Interview) and their own rather brittle, even aggressive, sophistication. By riding in on motor scooters and wearing trousers on their first appearance, the women seemed more 'male' than the men who had by that time changed into caftans. The long Indian robes reflected their attempts to become disciples, committed (like the King) to a particular way of life, but also a kind of feminisation, a reversal of stereotypes which Kahn had deliberately sought (Interview). Visually the women became the hunters, as indeed they are in IV.i, but then reverted to more customary women's roles, and costumes, in the final scene when they appeared in 'rather traditional, pastel, long gowns' (Cooper, p. 141). So the presentation of the central characters seems to include switches of gender roles, but only to a limited extent.

Kahn himself has wondered if the 'transposition' was as successful for the more comic characters, although he had no question about the Boyet/Truman Capote look. He admitted that Armado is 'a melancholy Quixote-like Spaniard' whose presence in India was difficult to rationalise; conceiving him as 'the last of the Edwardians' attended by 'a little Indian boy (Sabu)' is the closest he came to finding a place for a character who is already out of place (Interview). Other transpositions included Holofernes as Gandhi, Sir Nathaniel as 'an English Parson', and Dull as 'An Indian Policeman'. Kahn's comments in our conversation about his lack of success in finding an equivalent for Armado in his chosen setting imply that he was looking for a kind of consistency which he did not attain. But it is also possible to argue that the inconsistency is really eclecticism, and that, as in Brook's production and in Brook's theoretical statements, the text offers variety which can well be expressed through 'inconsistency'.

In creating his character transpositions, Kahn also created a time warp, since his central couples dressed in clothes that came directly from current fashion magazines, while the other characters seemed to belong to several earlier eras: the first decade of the twentieth century when a pre-war sense of order and empire still existed, and then the post-war 1920s and 1930s when Gandhi's independence movement threatened British control of India. But while the contemporary characters were only intermittently satirised, the British colonial characters became pure caricature. Kahn added American caricatures as well, again from different eras. The Forester was a version of 'Ernest Hemingway', while both Costard and Jaquenetta were American hippies (prompt-book descriptions). Jaquenetta chewed bubble gum throughout (as the personal properties list attests) while Costard sported a wildly curly hairdo, a 'screaming' yellow jacket (Beckerman, p. 308) and pants, a brightly flowered shirt, and a button reading 'Don't Squeeze the Banana'. In a production relatively faithful to the text, Costard got the interpolations: as Dull and Berowne carried Costard off at the end of the first scene, he shrieked 'Police Brutality, Police Brutality!' and when Moth kicked him as he was about to exit in I.ii he followed "therefore I will say nothing' with 'Fascist Hindu'. Since Kahn began rehearsing the production in the spring of 1968, presenting it first to student audiences (mid-March to early June) and then in the regular Festival season in late June, he could not have foreseen that 'Police Brutality' would echo to sinister effect for audiences seeing the production, as I did, in late August 1968. Then, coming out of the theatre, one heard reports from Chicago and the Democratic National Convention that made 'police brutality' a reality rather than a joke.

Inside the theatre, however, a spirit of light-hearted gaiety prevailed. While the obvious take-off of well-known figures created a pleasantly irreverent though still glamorous world, the characters themselves developed their own brand of humour, often verging on slapstick, but still tied to the language of the play. Costard was a case in point. He carried a long flower with him, and when he defended himself, 'As it shall follow in my correction' (I.i.210), he beat Dull with the flower. The contradiction between the familiar 1960s slogan 'Make Love Not War' and his actions became clear when he turned upstage, revealing that slogan stencilled on the back of his jacket; the movement occurred as the King attempted to shush him with 'Peace' and Costard cut him off with 'Be to me and every man that dares not fight.' The flower came into play again at the end of the scene, as he waved it in front of his crotch proclaiming 'Welcome the sour cup of prosperity' and then made it wilt on 'sit thee down, sorrow'.

Costard also sent others into comic behaviour, as at the end of III.i when Berowne, rhapsodising about Rosaline ('a gentle lady; / When tongues speak sweetly, then they name her name, / And Rosaline they call her', III.i. 159-61) put his arm around Costard's shoulder and then felt his 'breast' as if forgetting who he was actually speaking to. Costard, of course, did not let this opportunity slip by but put his ever-useful flower in his mouth and 'flirted' with Berowne. For such a character, smoking marijuana while listening to Nathaniel read the letter in IV.ii was a deliberate challenge – what better time than with the authority figures around? Such a Costard was not sympathetic when Nathaniel/Alexander forgot his lines in the Pageant, but spanked the sheepish-looking curate and moved to centre stage, perhaps about to take over from him, until the Princess said 'Stand aside, good Pompey' (V.ii.582). And when Armado, hearing Costard reveal that Jaquenetta is pregnant, asked indignantly 'Dost thou infamonize me among potentates?' (V.ii.670) he received a nod and a wide grin from Costard.

The jokes for Armado were more strained, perhaps reflecting Kahn's sense that he could not really find a 'type' for Armado in the contemporary setting in the same way that he had for others. Of course, while Costard was usually in control of what goes on around him (mixing up the letters was, in this production, the only exception, and he started to sneak away when he realised his mistake), Armado was almost always the butt of the jokes. Kahn emphasised the difference between Armado and Costard by having Armado enter (in I.ii) with a long-stemmed flower too; by the end of the scene he threw the flower to a giggling Jaquenetta. But before that point, he became a dummy dressed on stage by Moth and then mimicked a 'bull' charging at Moth who played the bullfighter with Armado's scarf as his cape – perhaps enacting visually 'Thou heat'st my blood' (I.ii.29-30). For a moment, he was a conqueror swinging his blade, 'I do excell thee in my rapier as much as thou didst me in carrying gates' (I.ii.69-71), and almost decapitating Moth who fell back on the floor; rapt in his contemplation of Samson, 'Who was Samson's love, my dear Moth?' (I.ii. 71-2), he unconsciously put the tip of his sword on Moth's belly. A second later, Moth moved the tip of the sword to Armado's foot, literally stabbing him even as his matter-of-fact answer, 'A woman, master' undercut his fantasies. Armado's almost monosyllabic conversation with Jaquenetta put him at even more of a disadvantage since she carried a portable radio to which she was listening

[84]

instead of him. First he pulled it away from her ear, then from her other ear. He ended up saying 'I love thee' to the radio, and, realising his mistake, repeated the line to Jaquenetta. The prompt book records an even sillier variation for the student season run of the production. Armado said 'I love thee' to Jaquenetta, heard the music from the radio which he had taken away from her, put the radio to his ear, and began to dance.

In his second appearance (III.i, end of the first act in Kahn's production), Armado continued to look like a mechanical doll with whom Moth illustrates the lines. When Moth launched into a shortened description of love's 'compliments' and 'humours' (III.i.9-20) he had but to say 'to jig off a tune at the tongue's end' for Armado to start singing 'Tiptoe through the tulips'. The incongruity of the song (made famous, or infamous, by the 1960s performer, Tiny Tim) coupled with Armado's impressive bearing (the actor, Josef Sommer, also played John of Gaunt that season) demonstrated the catastrophic effects of love on Armado. Moth illustrated 'canary to it with your feet' and then he and Armado danced offstage, crashing into each other as they tried to dance back to centre stage. The lines, 'with your hat penthouse-like o'er the shop of your eyes, with your arms crossed on your thin-belly doublet like a rabbit on a spit, or your hands in your pocket like a man after the old painting' were all enacted by Armado; he put his hat down over his eyes, then crossed his arms and stamped like a flamenco dancer, and ended up searching helplessly for non-existent pockets. When Moth 'proved' to Armado 'By heart you love her' (III.i.39) he became a teacher, holding up first one finger, and then another – each time Armado imitated him. While some actors, notably Paul Scofield in Brook's production, have stressed the melancholy side of Armado, Josef Sommer, under Kahn's direction, stressed an Armado made not just giddy, but even silly, through love, willing to try anything which might – or so he imagined – make him look like a lover.

Such an approach to Armado is, of course, consonant with the play's overall satiric tone. Interestingly, Kahn cut some of the insults to Armado when he presented Hector but substituted that familiar gag, the recalcitrant helmet whose visor 'blinded' Hector when he mentioned the 'armipotent Mars' and which Armado put on backwards when he tried to start his presentation again with 'This Hector far surmounted Hannibal' (V.ii.662). Indeed, Armado's physical clumsiness became a running joke, from early scenes where he almost hit Moth or bumped into him, to the chaos of his challenge of Pompey, where he swung at Costard and hit Moth instead and then, a moment later, accidentally hit the King on the jaw and knocked him flat when he proclaimed, again to Costard, 'By the north pole, I do challenge thee' (V.ii. 685). Given this kind of slapstick, it is not surprising that Dumaine and Longaville actually pulled off Armado's jacket so that it hung about his wrists, revealing that he wore a vest, but, as he confessed, 'no shirt'. And the final joke of the production was on him: rising to dismiss the audience with 'You that way', he then turned upstage on 'we' to indicate the characters and discovered that the four pairs of lovers had already gone. So, with a shrug, he continued the line, 'we this way', pointed upstage, and bowed as the stage went to blackout.

Just as Armado became incapacitated by love, so too the King turned into a physical and mental incompetent. The prompt book's notation for the entrance of Navarre in II.i is 'Long pause – "Love at first sight"' and was emphasised in this production not by a gong but a chord on the sitar. While Berowne crossed over to the motor scooter by which Rosaline was standing and tried to engage her in conversation, 'Did not I dance with you in Brabant once?' the King, still looking at the Princess even though he was trying to read the letter from her father, tripped up on to the second platform. The King's clumsiness came from his feelings, while in contrast Berowne fell off the scooter because Rosaline punctuated her line, 'Not till it leave the rider in the mire' (II.i. 120) by bumping him with her hip. Back in conversation with the Princess, the King had to resort to hasty mental subtraction to figure out 'yet there remains unpaid / A hundred thousand more' (II.i. 133-4). He ended the encounter by handing the Princess a flower (the gesture linking him with Costard and, more fatally for his vow, Armado), then bowed, 'Thy own wish wish I thee in every place' (II.i.178) and backed into Berowne. With a giggle, the King exited, followed by Dumaine and Longaville, leaving the downstage area to Berowne and Rosaline for another encounter.

But while most of the production mocked the idea of love, the lyrics of Moth's song 'Love, sweet love', heard first at the beginning of III.i, and then repeated for the curtain call, offered a gentler, if more syrupy, view. In the song 'Love is soft and warm and tender / Like a blanket of down, / It surrounds a world of splendour, / That lovers wear like a crown.' Love was also, metaphorically, 'a playful kitten, / One that's not very tame', 'a trip through time and space', and 'a portrait of a beautiful face'. The reprise of Moth's song for the curtain call also lent a hopeful note to the play's ending, just as the exits of the four sets of lovers implied that they were together rather than separate. As the last verse of Winter's song began, the King and Princess joined hands, crossed upstage and exited together. They were followed by Berowne and Rosaline, also with hands joined, then by Longaville and Maria, and then by Dumaine and Katherine. Although those exits set up the final joke on Armado, they also suggested that the waiting period will certainly end with multiple marriages.

Those marriages looked much less likely in the moments preceding the final songs. Marcade's entrance came in the middle of a comically busy scene, or, as the prompt book has it, 'Chaos again breaks loose.' Boyet pulled the treasured dishclout of Jaquenetta's not from Armado's heart, as the text suggests, but 'from behind Armado's backside' (prompt book). Marcade entered through the bamboo curtain which was brought on at the beginning of the Pageant and placed on the centre platform; each of the two ambassadors accompanying him crossed around that curtain and moved to a downstage corner of the second level of platforms, while Marcade stayed on the central platform. The improvisational horseplay was so riotous that no one noticed him until he spoke, 'God save you, madam' (V.ii. 707) and *then*, they all turned towards him and froze in position. The Princess crossed away from him, to an isolated position downstage left as soon as she heard 'The king your father – ' (V.ii. 711), while lighting cues implied a darkening stage. The conversations between the King and the Princess, Dumaine and Katherine, and Longaville and Maria all ended with the men moving downstage right (on the second platform), and the women downstage left so the implication of the stage picture was separation, not togetherness.

The movements in the last conversation of Berowne and Rosaline underscored the coming separation. Berowne, down centre on the bottom platform, took Rosaline's hand when he entreated her: 'Behold the window of my heart, mine eye' (V.ii. 830). At first he thought her words are positive, as she calls him

> a man replete with mocks;
> Full of comparisons and wounding flouts,
> Which you on all estates will execute
> That lie within the mercy of your wit. (V.ii.835-8)

Berowne, says the prompt book, 'is basking in Rosaline's praise' until the line 'To weed this wormwood' (839) lets him know that her words are not praise at all. He crossed away from her, objecting 'Mirth cannot move a soul in agony' (849), and she followed him, but he kept his back to her. *She* had to make all the moves, first touching his cheek when she said 'And I will have you and that fault withal', and then taking her hand away with 'But if they will not' (858, 859). Still he didn't look at her until she finished her speech, and then his words accept her terms although the physical action, as they crossed away from each other, belied that acceptance. Even while listening to Spring and Winter the couples remained separate, the men stage right, the women stage left, on the uppermost platform. The dark side of the play thus appeared primarily in the last ten minutes, and then was swept away in the exuberance of the final songs, especially the reprise of 'Love sweet love'.

A similar contrast in tone, between the farcical and the serious, occurred twice earlier in the play, both times with long speeches of Berowne. His soliloquy at the end of III.i. – the end of the first act in this production – came after Berowne's 'flirtation' with Costard. Unlike the detailed account of business throughout the prompt book, the note reads simply 'takes stage' – and that is what happened. The audience hears a man speaking, thinking – and because the actor, Lawrence Pressman, works directly with the audience, not posing or creating a persona, they listen. The same tonal shift, from extremes of comedy to straightforward seriousness, occurs near the end of IV.iii when the men ask Berowne to justify their change of heart. Given the excesses of this scene, from the rock-and-roll sonnets to Berowne's kneeling to kiss the ground in honour of Rosaline, to the incipient fight between Berowne and Dumaine, it is almost a shock to find that someone will just stand and speak. Once again the prompt book reads 'takes stage' and once again the character forces the audience to listen. Instead of the simple, and vapid, metaphors of 'Love sweet love', Berowne's and Shakespeare's eloquent praise of love rings out. All fifty-five lines of the speech (minus, of course, the uncancelled repetition) are there, and suddenly Berowne is serious. If only the mood could last, one thinks, or if only Rosaline could hear him, she would find more than just a man 'replete with mocks'. The clarity of his thinking lasts until the next-to-last line of the scene, 'Light wenches may prove plagues to men forsworn' (IV.iii. 381) as the King, Dumaine and Longaville step back from Berowne in shock; but then the gaiety of the production reasserts itself and the men exit 'wildly – much hoop-la'.

Reaction to the production was, as Roberta Cooper makes clear (pp. 142-3), decidedly mixed, ranging from those who found it appalling to those who enjoyed it greatly, and, in between, those who, like Bernard Beckerman, applauded the idea but not the execution. As Cooper points out, mod-rock versions of Shakespeare were current at the time, including the British *Catch My Soul*, based on *Othello*, and the American *Your Own Thing*, based on the main plot of *Twelfth Night*, the latter opening on Broadway in January 1968 (Cooper, p. 143). But Kahn's approach to the play reflects more than contemporary theatre trends. As his comments to me and to Ralph Berry make clear, he wanted to have his version of *Love's Labour's Lost* 'deal with *ideas* of the play' (Kahn, Interview). He has argued that 'a play helps say something a little more at a given moment, or, much more true of Shakespeare, a play helps you investigate something that you know is concerning you' (Berry, *On Directing Shakespeare*, p. 85). Kahn had first come to Stratford, Connecticut, in 1967, to a place which seemed to him 'superficial, chi-chi … . lightweight' (Kahn, Interview). In 1968, his second season, Kahn directed both *Richard II* and *Love's Labour's Lost*; the first production, with actors wearing costumes as 'traditional' as those of *Love's Labour's Lost* were contemporary, nevertheless could be seen as raising the question of the 'nature of leadership to a country embroiled in an increasingly unpopular war and with a president who had chosen not to run again' (Cooper, p. 139). Though *Love's Labour's Lost* had no such overt, or covert, political references, it did, interestingly enough, feature a society that one might call both superficial and lightweight. Thus it was a production implicitly critical of its immediate surroundings as well as the international fascination with cult figures.

Yet Kahn's primary motivation was to try to find for an audience in 1968 a series of visual references which would evoke a comic world of glamour, wealth, and intellectual pretension. The decision to use music was, as earlier productions of many of the plays had shown, a familiar one – and one which continued. In 1971, Joseph Papp's New York Public Theatre would make *The Two Gentlemen of Verona* into a rock musical, while in 1976, Trevor Nunn and the Royal Shakespeare Company turned *The Comedy of Errors* into a musical romp. Late seventeenth- and early eighteenth-century productions frequently added music to the better-known plays, and even to the tragedies (the infamous chorus of flying witches in Davenant's *Macbeth*, for example). Thus in 1968, Michael Kahn and the American Shakespeare Festival were following a long-standing tradition, even if they did not know about the opera Garrick had commissioned back in 1771 – and even if their production looked decidedly non-traditional.

Similarly, the use of modern dress for a production is certainly not new in the history of Shakespearean production; indeed for many years costumes contemporary to the period of the audience were the norm. But Kahn's work with a play which, in the twentieth century, seemed 'three hundred years out of fashion' (Granville-Barker, p. 1), was new. What made this production special was not so much its particular equating of the Beatles with the courtiers or the King of Navarre with the Maharishi, but its high-spirited approach to the play as a satire on contemporary affectations. By using fashions in clothes and in music as visual and aural equivalents of fashion in language, the production both exemplified Granville-Barker's description of *Love's Labour's Lost* as a 'fashionable play' and challenged his assertion that it was 'out of fashion'. In so doing, Kahn was responding not only to the play but to the concerns of the day, as he explained to Ralph Berry in the late 1970s:

> When I did *Love's Labour's Lost* in 1968 I was concerned with manners – we seemed to be in a time of superstars of one form or another whose fame was really based upon personality and modes of behaviour. That's not true right now, and *Love's Labour's Lost* does not interest me now. I think it's a beautiful play, but I would not be drawn to *Love's Labour's Lost* now, whereas in 1968 we were involved in the Beatles and the Onassis and the Kennedy ladies and Lee Radziwill and Mia Farrow and Truman Capote, and we had a series of pop stars and jet-setters, which I think was really the germ for Shakespeare's writing it too. It fascinated me, but it wouldn't now, because the era of media pop stars is over. (*On Directing Shakespeare*, p. 85)

Kahn's approach, as he makes clear throughout the interview with Berry, is not simply one of finding a modern equivalent for Shakespeare's language but of creating a vivid picture of 'one's relationship to the world at that given moment, as to what concerns one the most' (p. 84). One could well argue that Kahn's sense of the play as dependent on the contemporary fascination with superstars is in itself a dated view. But the notion that a production of a Shakespeare play *should* speak directly to the audience which sees it is one that has characterised Kahn's own work and thinking. In

England, Michael Bogdanov is perhaps the best-known director with such an approach, willing to create a new version of the Induction to *The Taming of the Shrew* (Stratford-upon-Avon, 1978) in order to underscore the tension between male and female power, or willing to move the Prologue of *Romeo and Juliet* (Stratford-upon-Avon, 1986) to the end of the play, to suggest the uselessness of the deaths and the falseness of the text's reconciliation between the families.

The year after his production of *Love's Labour's Lost*, Kahn directed *Henry V* for the American Shakespeare Festival, an even more controversial production dominated by its insistent metaphor of playground games and war games. The French wore huge padded costumes and stalked about on metal platform shoes, thus appearing to be gigantic and menacing. Downstage, translators spoke Shakespeare's lines in a microphone while the French spoke in French. Brechtian sur-titles were created for each scene. That production can be read as a response to the times, particularly in a United States still enmeshed in the increasingly meaningless Vietnam War. But Kahn also owed much to Goddard's ironic reading of *Henry V*, a defiantly post-World War II reading that questions the St Crispin's Day speech by doubting 'extreme protestations of democracy from those in high position if uttered at a moment when national safety depends on the loyalty of those of lower situation' (p. 246). Goddard speaks also of the irony of the wooing of Katherine, and Kahn's sur-title for the final scene was 'The Deal'.

Both productions forced audiences to re-evaluate the plays, just as Michael Bogdanov's have done, if only through irritation. Though *Henry V* seems to me a much richer play than Kahn's ironic production implied, I agree with Peter Smith's contention that 'the great value of this uneven and sometimes exasperating production was that it opened the debate in one's mind' (Smith, p. 450). Similarly, though *Love's Labour's Lost* seems to me more than a satirical play, the 1968 production made clear the pretensions about love that these characters cherish. By turning linguistic jokes into jokes about extravagant clothes and comically awkward movement, Kahn risked over-simplification but gained immediacy and exuberance. And yet, in those moments when Berowne 'took the stage', the production suggested, by letting the words speak without visual embellishment, the power of love to transform the silliness into something more lasting.

[91]

CHAPTER VI

Spring and Winter: Stratford-upon-Avon, 1965 and 1978

'John Barton's *Love's Labour's Lost* (RSC Stratford) is one of those productions which re-draw the map of a play. You thought you knew this one; a light, sharp piece; elegant, precious and self-conscious' (*The Sunday Times*, 13 August 1978). Whether critics argued, as John Peter did, for new discoveries, or proposed, as Robert Cushman did, 'not so much a discovery of unknown riches as a clear demonstration that those in which we always believed do actually exist' (*The Observer*, 20 August 1978), they found much to praise in John Barton's 1978 production at the Royal Shakespeare Theatre. Cushman describes the production's story:

> a play about four undergraduates who forsake the world because they are afraid to face it, are thrown by the arrival of four ladies, try to get the love-game together, are made ludicrous by the disclosure of their pretensions, try to put a good face on things, think they have succeeded and are defeated by the arrival of an unalterable reality, Death. (*The Observer*, 20 August 1978)

Cushman's suggestive reading of motive and action – 'who forsake the world because they are afraid to face it' – points to one of the major strengths of the production, the creation of characters who speak in 'elegant, precious and self-conscious' language not because *Shakespeare* is writing such language but because *they* are showing off, or defending themselves against feeling, or trying to communicate but tying themselves in knots while doing so.

Guiding actors to make the language reveal their feelings, or to serve as the cover for those feelings, is, of course, a Barton speciality, as Trevor Nunn makes clear in his introduction to the published text of Barton's television series, *Playing Shakespeare*. Nunn collaborated with Barton on a 1965 production of *Henry V* and describes his experience:

> I had always thought of Henry V as a role full of splendid and necessary rhetoric. Under John's direction, the mighty 'set speech' we know as Crispin's Day, for example, became the spontaneous, almost desperately improvised attempt by a young leader to hold the morale of his men together as they stared at inevitable defeat; and instead of there being any sense that the actor was delivering a previously written text, Ian Holm, as Henry, thought and discovered those words out of the situation and out of his character. Every clue of where to breathe, what to stress, when to run on, what to throw away was there in the text, if only like John you knew what to look for. But the poetry was not an end in itself. The words became necessary. (Foreword, *Playing Shakespeare*, p. viii)

Nunn's description of the words as *necessary* is central to Barton's approach, an idea which Barton stated frequently during the television programmes, as well as in rehearsal comments and public question-and-answer sessions:

> We can put this idea in various ways: we can say you've got to *find* them or *coin* them or *fresh-mint* them. We can use any word we want to describe the idea of inventing a phrase at the very moment it is uttered. The vital thing is that the speaker must *need* the phrase. He must not think of such phrases as simply words that pre-exist in the text. They have got to be words that he finds as he utters them. (*Playing Shakespeare*, p. 18)

For the finding to take place, the actor must know what he or she is trying to do – what, in Stanislavsky's terms, the intention or objective is. One might consider, for example, the King's long speech in II.i after reading the letter from the King of France. It is not important for plot, since the financial issues never arise again; in that case, why does the King keep repeating the sum of 'a hundred thousand crowns' (II.i. 129, 134, 143, 144)? For Barton, the terms 'language' and 'character' often work together – and he emphasises what purely academic readers often forget, namely that an actor starts with the language and uses that as a way of finding the character. Thus the repetition suggested that the King is 'shy and nervous' (Hodgdon, p. 21); because he doesn't know how to cope with the situation or the Princess, he falls into repeating phrases. A play such as *Love's Labour's Lost* offers both opportunities and challenges to Barton's connection of language and character, since it is so much 'a great feast of language' and seems only remotely concerned with character development. Barton's achievement, in his two productions of the play at Stratford – and most fully in the second – was to find how the play's extravagant language can also reveal the hearts of the characters.

For his 1965 production of the play at Stratford, Barton wrote a programme note in which he commented on 'the Elizabethan's sensual and extravagant preoccupation with words' and pointed out how everyone in the play (except Dull) 'relishes the game and bangs words to and fro like tennis-balls'. But reviews of the production suggest that the pace of the speaking was 'measured and weighty' (*The Times*, 8 April 1965) and the relish of the language slowed into 'bludgeoning self-consciousness' (*Queen's Counsel*, 21 April 1965). John Russell Brown, writing about the season as a whole, saw company policies developing, including attention to language: 'Apparently the company has been taught to scrutinize every word in a play so that they know, always, what they are saying' (p. 111) and praised the energy in 'passages of verbal complexity' (p. 112). But he also suggested that while at times the company took things too lightly and too comically, at other moments they adopted a 'portentous style' (pp.112-13) which seemed to weigh down *Love's Labour's Lost* in particular. For Brown, Barton signalled from the beginning 'that a solemn recognition of death's inevitable demands is the final purpose of the performance' (p. 117), both in the style of the performances and in the 'tall, dark, tangled forms of giant yew hedges that flank the stage' (p. 116); thus both the verse-speaking and the set may have slowed down the game of language which Barton had described.

The box hedges and unleaved trees which seemed so ominous to Brown were, as the designer Sally Jacobs noted in the programme, echoes of the garden architecture for a large country house and part of the highly stylised visual effect of the 1965 production. The patterned tapestry of the women's dresses, the tight blonde swirls of Glenda Jackson's wig as the Princess of France (see Figure III), the straw floor-covering which served as the greensward, and the huge hobby-horse carriage on which the Muscovites, dressed in elaborately woven long coats and immense furry hats, entered – all suggested a world dominated by formality and artifice. In such costumes, and against such a setting, the moments of 'natural' behaviour often seemed imposed, such as the King of Navarre's occasional use of spectacles (visible only in a few photographs and mentioned in several reviews, usually not with approval) or the reduction of Armado to a 'pathetic old man' (*Financial Times*, 8 April 1965) to which some reviewers objected because they expected a more flamboyant character, the 'fantastical Spaniard'. A more successful re-reading of character was that of Boyet, not as an affected fop but as 'an indulgent uncle' (*The Times*, 8 April 1965) who 'appears before us magisterial, not to say seigneurial, tall, ample, rubicund, bright assessing eyes watching beneath springing silver hair, fond of his young ladies and not above a pat or two' (*The Sunday Times*, 11 April 1965). But then, the actor was Brewster Mason, with two years of playing the magisterial manipulator, Warwick, in Hall and Barton's *The Wars of the Roses* (1963-64), and his imposing physical presence to serve him well. Indeed, the play's closing lines went to Boyet, clearly the authority figure of this production, rather than to Armado or, as in Brook's production, the Princess.

Other factors, outside the artistic decisions of director and designer, may have contributed to the relative 'stiffness' of the 1965 production. *Love's Labour's Lost* was the season opener on 7 April, followed quite quickly by Marlowe's *The Jew of Malta* on 14 April (transferring from the Aldwych) and *The Merchant of Venice* on 15 April. Since both Shakespeare productions depended on the presence of William Squire, who was to play Armado and Antonio, it was unfortunate that Squire fell and cracked his spine one day before the opening night of *Love's Labour's Lost*. His understudy, Stanley Lebor, had one preview before taking over Armado while Brewster Mason stepped in as Antonio, and reviewers clearly were not sure whether they were seeing the Armado imagined by Barton or just the pale version that the understudy could present. In contrast, Barton's 1978 production was the fourth show of the Stratford season, opening in August, after productions of *The Tempest*, *The Taming of the Shrew*, and *Measure for Measure*. Most of the cast had thus been working together at least half a year by the time the production opened.

Even more crucial than timing were choices Barton made about characters, both in terms of casting and relationships, when he directed the play again in 1978. And of those choices, none was more significant than the decision to cast Richard Griffiths as the King of Navarre. Certainly no one would have guessed – given his work as Bottom, Trinculo, and Pompey – that he would play what amounts to the second romantic lead in the production. Griffiths is a somewhat stout actor with glasses who seems an ideal choice for Holofernes or Nathaniel. But by choosing him to play the King, Barton not only worked against aristocratic stereotypes (Warren, p. 208), but made utterly plausible the notion that the King creates the academy and the oath as an attempt, albeit an unconscious one, to escape from a world in which he does not function easily. This man is congenitally uncomfortable around women, as his flustered responses to Costard show. Instead of a stern reproach to the cheeky young man, Griffiths's King is like a hesitant schoolmaster. When he points out, 'It was proclaimed a year's imprisonment to be taken with a wench' and receives Costard's rationalisation, 'I was taken with none, sir; I was taken with a damsel', the King is almost nonplussed. 'Uh', he ponders, and then remembers, 'Well, it was proclaimed damsel' (I.i. 280-4). The moment of *having* to remember is central. Dithering characterises the King, whether with Costard or with the Princess, except for one extra-textual moment when the men return after their Muscovite masquerade. The King is playing around with his sword, holding it by the hilt and pressing the tip into the ground, almost the way a tennis player unconsciously bounces a ball on his racket. He complains about Boyet, 'A blister on his sweet tongue, with my heart / That put Armado's page out of his part' (V.ii.335-6), and as he ends the couplet, he gives a little touch to the sword so that it jumps into the air, reverses itself, and comes down hilt first. Everyone is surprised at this neat trick; and indeed, at the first previews, the King's own reaction was a somewhat startled 'how did I do that?' look. By opening night, he took it in stride, shrugging a bit casually at his moment of triumph.

While Griffiths is physically different from Michael Pennington (Berowne), Ian Charleson (Longaville) and Paul Whitworth (Dumaine), and almost cuddly, he nonetheless sets the tone for the group of young men. To some extent they all share his modest taste in clothing (no silks or satins, but suede jackets, trousers, boots), his messy hair-style, his casual manner. Not only does the oath seem less pretentious – because it clearly comes from a delightfully naive and charmingly shy would-be academic – but Griffiths's nervous presence seems to make all of the men less inclined to show off through arrogant condescension. Berowne is, of course, more relaxed – though, one might argue, anyone would be more relaxed than this king – and perhaps because the King and his vow are such easy targets, he uses gentle irony rather than the rapier-like wit of the RSC's previous Berowne, Ian Richardson (in the

1973 production). For Michael Pennington's Berowne, wit is intelligent thinking rather than bravura performing, at least when he is with the other men. His choice to stay, against his better judgement, comes from his friendship for the King, 'I have sworn to stay *with you*' (I.i.111, emphasis mine), the friendship of a good-looking and clever man for a bumbling, but good-natured, one.

Barton combined this casting of the King with a reading of the Princess of France that also overturned previous conceptions of the play's leading lady, perhaps providing a suggestion to the 1984 casting of Maureen Lipman in the BBC version. Though Carmen Du Sautoy was not specifically identified with comic roles, as was Richard Griffiths, Ralph Koltai's costuming, especially the wig of long red ringlets, *and her glasses*, made her less than glamorous and, of course, identified her with the King. The key to this portrayal is the Princess's opening speech in which she discounts Boyet's praise of her beauty as 'painted flourish' (II.i.14). She knows that she is not beautiful and puts up with that kind of flattery because she has to. After Boyet leaves, the other women 'prepare' her for the meeting with the King (see Figure VI); Katharine arranges pearls in the Princess's hair, Rosaline kneels in front of her, brushing mud off her gown and her shoes, Maria sprays her with perfume (prompting a gesture of distaste from the Princess), and then hands her a mirror. The prompt book reads 'repulsed', but onstage the effect is 'I've no illusions', as she quickly looks and turns the mirror away. She is the kind of princess who *would* get mud on her dress and who probably would not do anything about it herself – a far cry from the carefully coiffed and elaborately gowned Princess of Glenda Jackson in 1965.

Du Sautoy's Princess and Griffiths's ·King are obviously meant for each other, and they fall in love almost at first sight. When she says 'suddenly resolve me in my suit', she holds out the letter and there is a long pause. He fumbles for words – 'Madam, I will, if suddenly I may' – and her answer, completely without sarcasm (a contrast to the acerbic tone of the BBC's Maureen Lipman at this moment), sounds as if she is struggling to put words together: 'You will the sooner that I were away' (II.i.110-11). Characteristically, as the King reaches out for the letter from her father, she accidentally drops it; both she and the King bend over to pick up the letter, the Princess gets it and hands it over to him, but both are embarrassed by the small mishap. He turns away to read the letter while she turns away – and takes off her glasses. The immediate falling in love of these two slightly clumsy and unromantic-looking people becomes very touching and creates a gentle tone for their relationship.

The sources for these readings of the King and Princess, so different from the elegant and usually self-assured rulers found in other productions, are varied. One source was clearly Griffiths himself, and his presence in the company. Barbara Hodgdon suggests, in her revealing study of the rehearsal process for the production, that Barton may have chosen Griffiths either as a version of his younger Cambridge self (when Barton played the King of Navarre) or as 'a deliberate contrast to his [Barton's] own persona' (p. 15) But when one looks back to the 1965 production, the occasionally-seen spectacles of Charles Kay's King seem prophetic, and Barton's 1965 programme note describing the Princess as 'shy, in some awe of the King, and none too sure about how to cope with any situation' now seems to apply even more to the King himself (Warren, p. 208). While, on the surface, such readings seem to contradict Barton's notion of the relish for the game of words, they actually support Barton's oft-expressed theory that the character must find the words as he or she needs them. People who are not easily witty will take the time to search for those words, and to value them.

A seemingly minor episode reveals the usefulness of Barton's choice to make the Princess and the King fall in love right away, and also to have the Princess be shy about her chances of succeeding with the King. At the beginning of IV.i, the Princess teases the Forester about his praise of her as 'fair' and then 'not fair'. Given her earlier rejection of Boyet's praise, her lines, 'What, what? First praise me, and again say no? / O short-liv'd pride! Not fair? alack for woe!' (IV.i.14-15) might well seem contradictory, as could her self-praise, 'I thank my beauty, I am fair that shoot' (IV.i.11). In 1965, with a blonde and pretty Princess, none of these lines remained in the acting text, perhaps because they sound rather conceited, as if the pretty girl is asking for more compliments and even praising herself. In 1978, Berowne leaves the stage at the end of III.i, slapping his chest as he regretfully admits that 'Some men must love my lady and some Joan', and immediately the Princess, not wearing her glasses, runs in and asks 'Was that the king, that spurred his horse so hard / Against the steep uprising of the hill?' (IV.i.1-2). Disappointed to hear that it wasn't, she puts her glasses on, that gesture implying that she has been trying to manage without them in case she should meet the King. The conversation with the Forester grows out of her disappointment about not seeing the King and having to return soon to France; she is looking for some comfort, if only from the Forester, since she clearly is getting nowhere with the King. Her decision, a few lines later, first to go ahead with the hunting and then not to hunt also reflects her need for praise:

> When, for fame's sake, for praise, an outward part,
> We bend to that the working of the heart;
> As I for praise alone now seek to spill
> The poor deer's blood, that my heart means no ill. (IV.i.32-5)

Such scrupulous self-awareness makes sense of the lines and grounds them in her character. Or one could argue that the character develops from the lines, that asking the question 'why does the character talk about these things?' leads to a sense that she is trying 'to mask her love for the King' (Hodgdon, p. 19).

Later in the same scene, Barton, like many directors, made Boyet's reading of Armado's letter into a leader-and-group-response activity. And, both in 1965 and in 1978, he invented a crucial Freudian slip for the Princess. Armado's description of the king and the beggar is couched in parallel phrases and then questions:

> he came, one; saw, two; overcame, three. Who came? the king: why did he come? to see: why did he see? to overcome. To whom came he? to the beggar: what saw he? the beggar: who overcame he? the beggar. The conclusion is victory: on whose side? the king's. The captive is enriched: on whose side? the beggar's. (IV.i.71-7)

As Boyet asks the questions, the women chime in with the answers – but on the last question, the Princess says 'the king's' while the others give the correct answer, 'the beggar's'. They all pause, realising that she is thinking about the King and then, with the help of the letter, Boyet plays directly to her, 'The catastrophe is a nuptial: on whose side? the king's' (IV.i.77-8), teasing her about her thoughts. Her cross away from the bench where Boyet has been sitting emphasises her need to hide her feelings, but Boyet follows her as he reads. The way in which the Princess reveals, sometimes unconsciously, what she feels demonstrates the extent to which the cast took to heart Barton's advice, 'Think Chekhov, not Elizabethan' (Hodgdon, p. 16). In Stanislavsky's *Creating a Character*, he asserts, 'Inside each and every word there is an emotion, a thought, that produced the word and justifes its being there', and describes how an actor must work imaginatively to create a 'score and inner image' such that 'the text will turn out to be the exact measure of the actor's creation' (p.94). Taking such an approach to *Love's Labour's Lost*, Barton and his cast found that seemingly abstract statements about praise or the comic reading of a letter could become, in a way that Chekhov and Stanislavsky would have admired, clues to the character's inner life.

The vulnerability of the Princess to her feelings for the King in no way lessens her feeling that the men's behaviour is something which requires major changes. In 1965 Barton had written that 'when the King and the rest break [the oath] at the first sight of a woman's eyes, the girls are justified in questioning their oaths of love', and then, as in 1978, he rearranged the text of V.ii to make that questioning even stronger. In 1965, the section when the men return in their own clothes after shedding their Muscovite costumes began as it does in the text, with the King inquiring for the Princess and Berowne (in a much cut speech) characterising Boyet. The women re-enter, and the first four lines of the text remain in sequence:

> *King*:   All hail, sweet madam, and fair time of day!
> *Princess*: Fair in all hail is foul, as I conceive.
> *King*:   Construe my speeches better, if you may.
> *Princess*: Then wish me better; I will give you leave. (V.ii.339-42)

Then, instead of the King's invitation, 'We came to visit you, and purpose now / To lead you to our court' (V.ii.344-5), both productions jump to the King's line 'O! you have liv'd in desolation here' (V.ii.357) and to the conversation about the Muscovites. (In 1965 there is even more rearranging, since Berowne's long speech, 'Thus pour the stars down plagues for perjury', gets moved to later in the scene.) The important textual decision in both 1965 and 1978 is to continue the scene with the King's 'Teach us, sweet madam, for our rude transgression/ Some fair excuse' (V.ii.431-2), to reveal the switched favours and misplaced oaths, and only *after* that exposure to return to the King's attempt to make everything all right by extending the invitation to visit at the court. But the Princess will not accept that invitation: 'This field shall hold me, and so hold your vow: / Nor God, nor I, delights in perjur'd men' (V.ii.345-6). She piles up the moral stakes as she speaks of 'virtue' and 'vice', of her 'maiden honour', and finishes with a resounding couplet, 'So much I hate a breaking cause to be / Of heavenly oaths, vow'd with integrity' (V.ii.355-6).

In 1978 the high moral tone of the speech contrasts with her action, for, as if to demonstrate her insistence in remaining 'in the field', the Princess picks up the broom that Rosaline used when she re-entered the stage (all of the women are ostentatiously doing something – 'the Princess peels carrots, Katharine weaves a basket, Maria plucks a chicken, Rosaline sweeps', reads the prompt book here) and begins to sweep the stage. Appalled, or infuriated, or both, the King takes the broom away from her, she tries to get it back, and this is the 'fair fray' which Costard interrupts with news about the Pageant of the Nine Worthies. By moving the section of text and adding the striking physical struggle, Barton focuses particular attention on it. Later, when the Princess rejects the King's offer of marriage by pointing out, 'your grace is perjur'd much' (V.ii.782), the verb reminds us of the anger earlier in the scene when she said 'Nor God nor I delights in perjured men', anger visible in her 'fight' over the broom as well in her voice. So her refusal is based not only on the immediate circumstances of hearing about her father's death, but on her previously voiced opinion that the King needs to learn how to take vows seriously.

Such textual rearrangement, while clarifying a particular interpretation of the text, does of course raise a major question about Barton's work. On the one hand, he emphasises the centrality of the text, and the usefulness of studying the text as a way of finding the character. But on the other hand, he seems not only willing, but even eager, to change the text, either by moving it around, or (not in *Love's Labour's Lost*, but in a number of other productions, notably *The Wars of the Roses*, 1963 and *King John*, 1974) by adding new lines, some of which he has written himself. The major rearrangement of scenes involved in turning the first tetralogy of history plays into *The Wars of the Roses* prompted much debate and elicited extended explanations from both Peter Hall and John Barton. One such explanation was that the plays themselves were not necessarily all by Shakespeare, and Barton advanced a similar explanation about *Love's Labour's Lost* when he spoke to Gareth Lloyd Evans in 1964, pointing out that the play 'contains parallel passages which clearly represent Shakespeare's own revision alongside earlier sections they were intended to replace' (quoted in Greenwald, pp. 83-4). Of course the flaw in this argument is that Barton does not contain his rearrangements simply to such passages in the text of *Love's Labour's Lost*, but makes changes to fit his ideas about characters and actions.

A possible understanding of the paradox might come from Barton's oft-repeated advice to the actor, '*make the words your own*' (Barton, *Playing Shakespeare*, p. 67). It is as if he applies that advice to himself, and once he feels he knows the play, he begins to make it his own and thus allows himself the liberty of reshaping it. The choice to reshape seems to come from a desire to clarify – whether the clarification is of motivation or of background. It is, admittedly, tampering, but of a highly intelligent kind, based on Barton's long experience with the texts, their sources, related plays, the practicalities of production, and the experience of rehearsals. While Barton certainly began his rehearsals of *Love's Labour's Lost* in 1978 with an already cut text (based, of course, on the 1965 production), he ultimately restored about 100 lines of the 400 he had originally planned to cut (cf. Hodgdon, pp.11-12).

Barton's textual changes to emphasise personal relationships apply to Berowne and Rosaline as well as to the King and Princess. In II.i, for the first meeting of the men and women, he takes the second Berowne/Rosaline set of stichomythic lines and moves them from just after the King's exit to the very end of the scene. In 1965, Maria, Katharine and Boyet leave and Rosaline is the last to go; Berowne appears from the opposite side of the stage, and the prompt book does not make it clear if she has lingered deliberately or not. In 1978, Rosaline stays behind deliberately, perhaps catching sight of Berowne hiding in the bushes. Instead of following the Princess, Katharine, Maria and Boyet out with her travelling bags and long cape, she removes the cape with a flourish, flings it on the bench and sits on it, one arm resting casually along the back of the bench, the very picture of controlled relaxation. Berowne has to come out of the bushes, and then we hear 'Lady, I will commend you to mine own heart' (II.i.179). In the text this exchange is relatively public, since everyone else is on stage, but Barton contrives this private meeting by transposing the lines, and thus emphasises their mutual attraction to each other (*he* has come back, *she* has waited for him), as well as Rosaline's cool wit. Jane Lapotaire also shows us a Rosaline fighting against his attractiveness, as she whips out a little penknife on a long cord when she replies to Berowne's line, 'Will you prick't [i.e. his heart] with your eye?' with 'No point, with my knife' (II.i.187-8). The studied attack seems not just aggressive but also carries with it a sexual connotation, and thus an implicit invitation. Even more noticeable is the warmth behind Berowne's 'Now, God save thy life!' and her equally warm response, 'And yours', before she remembers that she should not make this wooing too easy and adds 'from long living!' (II.i.190-1). The put-down sends him away, but she remains on stage until Boyet reappears, coughs meaningfully, and takes one of her pieces of luggage away. Alone, she picks up the other bag and her cape, and, before leaving, looks off stage in the direction Berowne has taken.

Rosaline's inner conflict about Berowne receives further emphasis from two other moments of textual fiddling. Early in V.ii she speaks of her desire to 'torture' Berowne, to 'make him fawn, and beg, and seek, / And wait the season, and observe the times, / And spend his prodigal wits in bootless rhymes' (V.ii.62-4). In Shakespeare's text, the Princess, Rosaline, and Maria pick up the last line, 'That he should be my fool and I his fate' (V.ii.68) and comment, somewhat abstractly, about folly. But Barton makes Rosaline's words the last we hear before Boyet enters to report on the coming of the Muscovites; he thus emphasises her attraction to Berowne but also her sense of wanting to control him, perhaps because she is afraid that she cannot. Then, near the very end of the play, Barton restores lines that are cut in almost every production of the play because they look like an uncancelled early draft. After the King hears from the Princess that he must spend a year in 'some forlorn and naked hermitage', most productions move directly to Dumaine's question to Katharine, 'But what to me, my love? But what to me? / A wife?' (V.ii.815-16), skipping over Berowne's question, 'And what to me, my love? and what to me?' and Rosaline's

> You must be purged to your sins are rack'd:
> You are attaint with faults and perjury;
> Therefore, if you my favour mean to get,
> A twelvemonth shall you spend and never rest,
> But seek the weary beds of people sick. (V.ii.809-14. The first line of the speech is sometimes emended to 'You must be purged, too, your sins are rank'.)

Since, later on, after Dumaine and Longaville receive their 'penances', Berowne again asks Rosaline to 'Impose some service on me for thy love' (V.ii.832) and receives a much expanded version of her lines in reply, it seems likely that Shakespeare forgot to cancel this version and decided to build up to Berowne and Rosaline rather than making them second in the list of four proposals and four refusals. But, by keeping Berowne's question and the first two lines of Rosaline's reply (V.ii.809-11), Barton emphasises the seriousness of her mood. In 1978 Berowne is sitting, legs stretched out in front of the bench, saying almost lightly, 'And what to me, my love?' (V.ii.809) in a tone that implies he'll have to do something, but it won't be very difficult. When Rosaline turns away, as if to think what his punishment should be, both Berowne and the audience are startled. And the echo of Berowne's line in Dumaine's question becomes a character cue, since Dumaine has always seemed the youngest and most naive of the men. What would he do in such a situation but follow Berowne's example? (A small extra-textual point underscores the notion of Dumaine watching Berowne, since, in 1978, Paul Whitworth, who played Dumaine, was the understudy for Michael Pennington's Berowne, just as in 1965, Michael Pennington played Dumaine and understudied Charles Thomas's Berowne.)

Even more important than the textual rearrangements is the shape of the Berowne/Rosaline relationship which these rearrangements sharpen for us. In Shakespeare's text, their relationship develops more quickly and directly than does that of the King and the Princess, who have no real 'scenes' together in which they can express their feelings; the two encounters in II.i, Berowne's soliloquy at the end of III.i, and his soliloquy at the beginning of IV.iii all focus attention on Berowne and Rosaline as the central pair of lovers. But just as Barton adds a physical conflict to the dialogue between the King and the Princess, so he does likewise for Berowne and Rosaline. This one also occurs in the last scene, during the frantic aftermath of Costard's revelation to Armado that Jaquenetta is pregnant. Armado, wearing his Hector costume, including cothurni [modelled on the Greek platform shoes worn in classical tragedy] a foot high, cannot move quickly, so the young men easily surround and tease him. Longaville grabs the cymbals which Jaquenetta has held and bangs them in Armado's ear, while Berowne grabs Armado's lance and attached pennon and runs around the stage crying 'More Ates, more Ates! stir them on! stir them on!' (V.ii.680-1). Such behaviour looks like playground bullying, but it feels even more uncomfortable because these men should be too grown up to behave in this way. Berowne's incitement of the fight makes utterly clear what all their interruptions have been about – the pleasure taken by the clever and the strong in humiliating the dull and the weak. Rosaline tries to stop him by seizing the lance, but he pulls away from her so violently that she falls to the ground.

Such 'wrestling' echoes that of the King and Princess and suggests just how much punishment it will take to 'cure' Berowne.

The frenetic atmosphere in which such behaviour seems believable has been building gradually since the beginning of the Pageant. It continues to build with the challenges by Pompey and Armado, Berowne's seizing of Armado's lance, the move by Dumaine to help arm Costard, and the attempt by Longaville and Moth to take off Armado's shirt. On the line, 'since when I'll be sworn he wore none but a dishclout of Jaquenetta's, and that a'wears next his heart for a favour' (V.ii.704-6), Moth pulls a dishcloth out of Armado's armour and tosses it to Costard, who throws it to Longaville. Longaville realises that they're playing 'keep away' and tosses the cloth to Sir Nathaniel; the puzzled cleric throws it to the Princess, who is standing on the bench. She doesn't know what to do with it, so she tosses it to Holofernes, who hastily throws it to Dumaine, who sends it back to Longaville, who tosses it upstage – and at this moment it is caught, up centre, by Marcade. The game stops as he drops the cloth disdainfully to the ground and comes down centre towards the Princess, who is perched, with bare feet, on the bench. The pose could scarcely be less queenlike, and that is a deliberate choice. One is never prepared for death, but to be found barefoot and playing a silly game is to heighten the lack of preparation – and the switch to silence. The Princess steps down from the bench, trying to find a place on a stage full of people where she can be alone with her grief; everyone kneels except for Armado, who cannot, and Berowne, who holds the lance.

Barton's invention of the game of 'keep away' works on various levels: it masks Marcade's entrance from the audience while simultaneously providing a wild and chaotic environment in which his announcement of France's death will come with maximum shock. Even more importantly, the cruelty of the game – since Armado is rather like a bear being baited, 'chained' by the ridiculous costume which keeps him from moving quickly – makes physical the verbal cruelty of the comments by the young men during the Pageant (the King is the noticeable exception, and he, significantly, does not take part in the 'keep away' game either). If we have had any question about the necessity for these young men to grow up, their behaviour during the Pageant and now during the game removes any such question. They certainly need to study – if not strictly academic subjects, then common humanity and decency.

Part of the impact of this whole last section of the play depends on the careful building of sympathy for the performers of the Pageant – Armado, Moth, Holofernes, Sir Nathaniel, and, to a lesser extent, Costard (who doesn't really need audience sympathy since he never seems at a loss). Just as he had done in 1965, Barton sought to create an Armado who combined dignity and absurdity. He was helped by the presence of Michael Hordern, who also played Prospero in the 1978 season, and who reminded reviewers of 'a dotty Quixote' (*Guardian*, 14 August 1978) or the White Knight from *Through the Looking Glass* (*Financial Times*, 14 August 1978). Armado's costume evoked both Don Quixote and a mendicant friar, with a metal breastplate (at first), a grey burlap robe (similar to the ones the young men will wear later), and grey rags for shoes. His quiet melancholy is emphasised by the pert, quick-witted Moth of Jo James – trim, dark-haired, and totally self-possessed – while Armado is untidy, greying, and constantly at a loss for the right thing to do or say. Barbara Hodgdon's notes on the rehearsal process include the revealing comment, 'Moth is a learned, clever little boy – very old, about 108. He thinks of Armado as a younger brother' (Hodgdon, manuscript). Because Hordern's Armado is, like the White Knight, always slightly somewhere else, lines such as 'Sirrah Costard, I will enfranchise thee' (III.i.117) sound noble rather than affected, part of a mental script he has read, or written, about how real knights speak – like Quixote quoting the romances he has read.

Just as Armado and Moth form an odd couple, so too do Holofernes (Paul Brooke) and Sir Nathaniel (David Suchet). In this production, what holds them together is Nathaniel's obvious appreciation for almost everything Holofernes says. But that appreciation extends to a tolerance for others as well, so that when Holofernes criticises Dull for not understanding his Latin phrase, 'haud credo', Nathaniel explains, 'Sir, he hath never fed of the dainties that are bred in a book' (IV.ii.23). As the kindly Nathaniel sees it, Dull simply lacks a proper education. Holofernes basks happily in Nathaniel's praise, and while he does condescend to Dull, gesturing to 'the sky, the welkin, the heaven' or to 'the soil, the land, the earth', he combines that condescension with the school-teacher's need to explain. Thus when Holofernes launches into '*Venetia, Venetia / Chi non ti vede, non ti pretia*' (IV.ii.93-4), only to get a blank stare from Costard, Holofernes explains, 'Old Mantuan, old Mantuan!' as if that will make everything clear. Of course

Holofernes hates being anything other than the centre of attention, so when Nathaniel reads the sonnet/letter which Costard and Jaquenetta have brought, he first sits by Nathaniel, but then rises, wanders upstage, and finally takes the letter away from Nathaniel to check for himself. When Holofernes and Nathaniel reappear in V.i, Nathaniel still adores everything Holofernes says – and has said, offstage. His praise sounds even funnier because it is so effusive:

> your reasons at dinner have been sharp and sententious; pleasant without scurrility, witty without affection, audacious without impudency, learned without opinion, and strange [Nathaniel pauses for breath, and Holofernes darts a questioning glance at him, so Nathaniel explains] without heresy. (V.i.2-6)

When Holofernes draws out the word 'per-e-grinate', Nathaniel takes out a little notebook and writes down that word, just as a few minutes later he will write down Armado's choice phrase 'the posteriors of the day' (V.i.81), once Holofernes puts the stamp of approval on the phrase by calling it 'well culled, chose; sweet and apt' (V.i.85).

By carefully establishing the personality and the essential likeability of each of the rustics, Barton sets up the Pageant as something we watch with sympathy as well as with amusement. Even the planning of the Pageant shows the gentleness of the characters. Though Holofernes has looked at Dull for a moment after assigning Hector to Armado (a bit of textual rewriting here to reflect the actual roles that the characters play in the following scene), he moves directly on to Costard as Pompey, the pause telling us that Dull will not be cast. But when they start to leave, Holofernes does turn to Dull and kindly invites him along, commenting 'thou hast spoken no word all this while'. Dull brings the house down with his reply, 'Nor understood none neither, sir' (V.i.139-41); but Holofernes, as if realising the problem, then says '*Allons*! we will employ thee' (V.ii.142). So no one will be excluded, and Dull agrees to play on the tabor.

The sympathy generated by the characters is particularly evident in Sir Nathaniel's attempt to present Alexander the Great. Costard has galloped around the stage, as Pompey, with a small white hobby-horse attached by shoulder-straps, but Sir Nathaniel pretends to ride a huge yellow and white horse, the long draperies covering the horse also hiding the actor's feet. In Barton's 1973-74 production of *Richard II* where the horse first appeared, it looked majestic, but here it almost dwarfs Sir Nathaniel. Moreover, he carries a long silver lance tipped with red and wears a helmet and a long black cape, so he enters slowly, of necessity. Once in position he carefully and painstakingly manoeuvres the long lance into an upright position. Facing the nobles, he begins his speech:

> When in the world I liv'd, I was the world's commander;
> By east, west, north, and south, I spread my conquering might: (V.ii.558-9)

He lets go of the horse's reins to hold up his shield, illustrating 'My scutcheon plain declares that I am Alisander' (V.ii.560). But this gesture is a disastrous mistake, for it means that his horse tips forward and he loses his balance. Slowly and inexorably the horse descends and he goes down with it – and the enormous lance comes down slowly as well: an exercise in comic slow motion with Nathaniel powerless to stop the descent. He keeps repeating his opening line, 'When in the world I liv'd, I was the world's commander' – the text gives him one repetition, but Barton adds another – in a voice increasingly frail and close to tears. By the second repetition he is almost invisible under helmet, shield, cape and horse; only his feet, scuffling helplessly, seem to respond to Costard's 'run away for shame, Alisander' (V.ii.574). Not until Costard finally removes his shield can Nathaniel slowly get out of the horse. At this moment, the Princess moves to help him by picking up his lance – and the King comes to help her. She looks at him happily, in a moment that reverses and erases their previous struggle over a much smaller 'lance', the broom; and they hand the lance back to Nathaniel before his exit.

Nothing else in the Pageant of the Nine Worthies stops the show quite so hilariously, but then nothing else blends the painful and the comic quite so thoroughly. The Moth-as-Hercules snake-strangling is likewise comic; the enthusiastic boy rolls around on the floor with the snake, briefly menaces the Princess with it, bangs its head on the ground and then, just in case, takes his Cerberus-killing club from Holofernes and hits the stuffed snake again. Holofernes has to hustle him off and then quickly climbs into his horse, another of the *Richard II* hobby-horses, but this one all in black. Holofernes, a bigger man than Nathaniel, rides his horse with aplomb, galloping in with such abandon that everyone has to duck to avoid his lance. Though he can manage his steed, bowing to the nobles and trotting around the stage, he cannot manage to keep the audience quiet until his reproof – 'This is not generous, not gentle, not humble' (V.ii.623) – tones down their laughter a bit. Boyet reaches forward and pats the horse on the nose in a gesture that looks faintly like an apology.

Thus, by the time Armado enters to a melancholy trumpet fanfare, with his helmet, cape, lance and cothurni, the Pageant has provided much hilarity and also moments of pain. 'The appearance of the black-clad Mercade in such a scene of merriment stops the heart' noted B. A. Young (*Financial Times*, 14 August 1978), seeing the interdependence which Barton so clearly created between the humorous and the painful. The pain is the reality which Marcade's entrance makes utterly clear. It is also the reality toward which the play has pointed us since our first view of the set. For this production, Ralph Koltai designed a set which combines the natural world with the stage world in a simple but effective way. A large rectangular platform of greyish wood, edged with brown, is the main acting area. It is, almost literally, a stage, and since it is slightly raked, people have to step up on to it when they enter. On it, stage left, is a huge branch of a tree, bent to form a bench. Bushes surround the sides of the platform, and downstage left, grow into a tree which Berowne will climb for the overhearing scene. The rest of the stage is a deep leafy park; there the stage floor is strewn with leaves, and when characters enter from upstage, they make their way through the park. The time is late summer turning into autumn, since the fallen leaves are in tones of browns, oranges, and golds, while the leaves on the trees are mostly green, though in places the autumn colours are visible.

The two parts of the set allow for the 'reality' of the park (without the formality of the topiary hedges that characterised Sally Jacobs's design for the 1965 production) and, simultaneously, an acting area on which people can pose and present themselves, as they constantly do in this play. Because the main platform is so clearly a stage, it becomes the place for the Pageant of the Nine Worthies as well – obviating the need for the kind of fit-up stage that the BBC production used or the mobile wagon which has been a familiar Stratford device; Barton used a 'vast double-decker shandrydan [a nineteenth century carriage]' (*Financial Times*, 8 April 1965) in 1965, while David Jones in 1973, and Barry Kyle in 1984, also used versions of the pageant wagon. Because the platform is a stage, we accept moments of stylised behaviour such as the choreographed popping in and out of the young men in II.i to ask the names of the women, or the formalised grouping which gives us, in scene after scene, the men stage right and the women, balancing them, stage left. Yet this 'empty space' is also surrounded by a wonderfully real, and lovely, wooded park. The two worlds intersect from the opening moments, when Jaquenetta and Costard and the Forester appear on the platform, sweeping leaves off it, then scurrying away when they hear the fanfare announcing the arrival of the nobles. We watch the men enter through the park, as later we will watch the Princess and her women enter (the Princess picks up some leaves and drops a few on Boyet's hat), and as, at the end, we will see the women leave the same way.

Such a blending of visual styles fits with the production's awareness of the various styles of the play and offers a design solution that allows for the existence of the real and the non-real, the natural and the artificial, in a happy balance. In earlier productions, the emphasis on the artificiality of the world seemed uppermost, from the balanced pavilions of Tyrone Guthrie to the symmetrically balanced stage of Peter Brook to the rigidly formal trees and hedges of Barton's 1965 production. Indeed, Sally Jacobs discussed her design for the 1965 production in terms of 'an enclosed world', and the pictures of her various models show that the set was bounded not just by the proscenium arch, but by painted flats which also closed in the acting space. But by opening up the side and back areas of the stage, making them a space which seemed to flow offstage into yet further wooded areas, Ralph Koltai gave Barton's 1978 production less rigidity and formality. Moreover, by making the trees light, airy, and leafy, rather than starkly bare as Sally Jacobs had made them for the 1965 production, Koltai managed to suggest the ending subtly (fallen leaves) rather than obviously.

The use of the platform also seems to provide a thematic comment, as it did in Barton's 1980 production of *Hamlet* (another Ralph Koltai design), where the stage contained an even larger wooden platform, surrounded by huge property chests from which armour and other hand props could be taken. The setting was obviously a 'stage' and thus reminded the audience constantly of 'acting' and 'playing', metaphors familiar from the text of the play, and emphasised in the production's programme note. At the play's end, Fortinbras's command, 'Let four captains / Bear Hamlet like a soldier to the stage', was the cue for picking up Hamlet's body (Michael Pennington again) and carrying it to the centre of the stage-platform; the final image was the spotlight on that body, the actor–prince taking his final curtain call. *Love's Labour's Lost* is less obviously self-conscious about acting than is *Hamlet*, but the platform reminded us of the many 'plays' that we see, especially in the play's long last scene, when the text becomes more self-reflexive than elsewhere. Berowne wants his wooing to 'end like an old play' (V.ii.866); his final words, on hearing that he must wait 'a twelvemonth and a day' are 'That's too long for a play' (V.ii.869, 870).

The last such 'play' is, of course, 'the dialogue that the two learned men have compiled in praise of the owl and the cuckoo' (V.ii.877-9). And on the wooden platform, surrounded by trees, Barton's production emphasised both the 'performance' and the reality. As in 1965, Barton insisted that the songs be spoken, not sung, thus avoiding any large 'production number' feel to the ending. Instead, the presentation was very much in keeping with the 'two learned men' – and in this case, rather gentle men – who have written it. The rustics gather around the bench, Holofernes and Nathaniel sitting on the upper limb, Costard, Jaquenetta and Dull on the lower part, with Armado standing upstage of them (see Figure VII). Down centre, the King and Princess sit together, while Berowne, Longaville, and Dumaine range themselves along the stage right side of the platform with their respective ladies opposite them, stage left. Nathaniel wears a green wreath (suggesting spring) around his neck and carries a small puppet of a cuckoo while Holofernes wears a similar wreath in brown and red (suggesting autumn, fading into winter) and carries an owl puppet. The mood is one of story-telling, with Nathaniel beginning quietly, 'When daisies pied and violets blue'. Holofernes picks up the tale with 'The cuckoo then on every tree', and Nathaniel does a gentle 'cuckoo' which the others join, except for Costard and Dull who say 'cuckold'. The second verse of 'Spring' follows the same pattern, except that this time the rustics try to get the King and the Princess to join them on 'cuckoo' – the King does, the Princess doesn't. For 'Winter,' Holofernes becomes the story-teller, with Nathaniel leading the chorus on 'Then nightly sings the staring owl'. Holofernes does his obviously well-known owl imitation, while, on the second verse, Dull adds a wind sound on the first line, and Costard hisses for the roasting apples. Suddenly, after the onstage audience has joined in on the owl noises, a real owl hoots – or, should we say, an offstage owl – and everyone looks up and listens. It sounds again in the still night and Sir Nathaniel says happily 'a merry note'. The words of the song/dialogue are magically appropriate, and it is this harmony between performance and the natural world which lends a quiet blessing to the play's ending of separation. The women leave through the park, the men leave stage right. Armado, now more than ever the Quixote figure, strumming his lute, moves towards his Dulcinea and then wanders off, so that lights come down on Jaquenetta lying under a bush, downstage left, playing 'he loves me, he loves me not' with the fallen leaves.

Barton's insistence on having the final songs spoken rather than sung bothered reviewers in 1965; Mary Holland complained of 'perversity, right to the very end when the last moving song of the Owl and the Cuckoo is declaimed as a speech' (*Queen's Counsel*, 21 April 1965) and the drama critic of *The Times* asked querulously 'what can have induced Mr. Barton to have the final songs spoken?' (*The Times*, 8 April 1965). No such reservations appeared in the 1978 reviews, perhaps because the productions differed so greatly in tone. In 1965, the presentation of the songs still partook of the elaborate artificiality that had characterised the play as a whole, and particularly the last scene with the huge hobby-horse cart for the Muscovites and the pageant-wagon for the Worthies. B. A. Young described the songs as 'recited by the villagers in front of great wickerwork models of a cuckoo and an owl with practical beaks and eyes, while a small band accompanies them at the back' (*Financial Times*, 8 April 1965). In 1978, the simplicity of the presentation, with hand puppets instead of large figures, no musical accompaniment but only the unexpected owl noise, and, most importantly, the joining in by the onstage audience, created a sense of community that gently reversed the details of the opening. Now, instead of acting as menials, sweeping the stage and leaving before the court arrives, the rustics are centre stage, and it will be the courtiers who leave. Jaquenetta was one of the three sweepers at the beginning, but it is she who remains at the end of the play.

The harmony which this ending produces between the courtiers and the rustics grows out of choices about the world of the play which downplay the sharp dividing line between court and rustics so noticeable in Peter Brook's production. Such blurring of class roles was similarly visible in the costuming for the BBC production. But whereas Moshinsky's production gave everyone surface elegance, and little heart, Barton's production emphasised the essential good nature and humanity of each character and downplayed the sense of elegance. The move away from elegance –

in set, in costumes, in the physical presence of the actors – marks a genuine change in the approach to the play that has dominated its production history. And I would suggest that this move makes it possible to believe – more than in other productions – that these men and women genuinely love each other. The 'love at first sight' decision can so often seem a cliché, but when played by Richard Griffiths and Carmen Du Sautoy, it becomes a touching moment, precisely because they look like people who have always wanted to be loved and who have never succeeded. Because their feelings, disguised by talk about political matters and the inconvenience caused by the King's oath, are nonetheless painfully clear, they make the audience feel that love can be more than 'a merriment'.

The Berowne/Rosaline relationship also reveals more genuine feeling than in many other productions, and here Barton's insistence on the immaturity of the men makes itself felt. The problem is not just the issue of making silly vows or of breaking oaths, but of using one's wit appropriately. By making Berowne ask not just once, but twice, what he must do to win Rosaline, Barton forces us to wait as well for her answer. Berowne's second try, 'Studies my lady? mistress, look on me' (V.ii.829), comes after a noticeable pause, and one feels that he has chosen the word 'studies' because it fits Rosaline's intense look of concentration. At first she moves away from him, down to the right-hand corner of the platform, and a change in lighting shadows the other couples, giving even more focus to Rosaline and Berowne. She is grave in look and in tone (see Figure VIII); and while Berowne at first smiles to hear her description of him, his smile soon turns into defiance and astonishment: 'To move wild laughter in the throat of death? / It cannot be; it is impossible: / Mirth cannot move a soul in agony' (V.ii.847-9). Rosaline responds immediately, almost fiercely, the speed of her reply and the sharp 'g' and 'b' sounds of 'Why, that's the way to choke a gibing spirit' (V.ii.850) adding to the attack. She crosses behind him, the movement giving her power, and he falls to his knees as she continues to explain, but not relent: 'A jest's prosperity lies in the ear / Of him that hears it, never in the tongue / Of him that makes it' (V.ii.853-5). We think, inevitably, of Berowne's high-spirited dashing around the stage with Armado's standard, and of the wrestling with the standard that ends up with Rosaline on the ground. At the end of the speech, she seems almost inviting, kneeling to face him when she says 'But if they will not, throw away that spirit' and gently touching his face on 'And I shall find you empty of that fault, / Right joyful of your reformation' (V.ii.859-61). Her tone and her gesture tell us that she loves him, but he remains bitter, with the phrase, 'A twelvemonth!' jumping out in surprise. He accepts her conditions but refuses to play the rhyme of 'well, befall what will befall, / I'll jest a twelvemonth in an hospital' (V.ii.862-3). By giving the last word its modern pronunciation, and thus rejecting the rhyme which the rhythm invites, he lets us feel, with him, his sense of disappointment. He tries to take Rosaline's hand, but she moves it away. In rehearsal, Hodgdon notes (p. 25), the exchange included a full embrace when Rosaline said 'And I will have you' (V.ii.858); in performance, their gestures anticipate that embrace but never achieve it. Love's labour, for the moment at least, is lost.

CHAPTER VII

'You that way; we this way'

John Barton's 1978 production stands not only as an extraordinarily rich and subtle reading of the play, but as a point from which we can assess the development of stage interpretations of *Love's Labour's Lost* in the nineteenth and twentieth centuries. Barton's quiet opening, with Jaquenetta, Costard, and the Forester sweeping the fallen leaves off the platform *before* the fanfare announcing the King and his nobles, is emblematic of the change from the much more elaborate openings of productions such as Brook's 'prologue' with the special curtain painted to announce the oath or the extended 'burial' ceremony devised by David Jones in 1973 when the King and his court solemnly abandoned their past lives. The understated opening in 1978 and the appearance of the four young men, without any attendants, luggage-carriers or flag-bearers, immediately established a world that seemed gentle and friendly rather than elegant or beautiful. To imagine such a world was Barton's achievement, but it is an achievement more possible, I would suggest, to a director who had already staged a more formal production in 1965. That earlier production, at least in terms of design, was one very much in keeping with others that had preceded it on the English stage, even while Barton's commentary on it suggested that he took the issue of oath-making and oath-breaking more seriously than other productions had done. The great step forward in 1978 seems to be Barton's freeing of himself from the 'prettiness' so long associated with the play, not just in terms of set and costume, but, more importantly, in terms of the physical presence of the actors (notably Richard Griffiths as the King and Carmen Du Sautoy as the Princess). Once the production developed a rather homespun look for its noble characters, the language sounded less like the witty badinage of sophisticated people and more like the attempts of immature people to impress each other.

In 1965, Barton wrote about the variety of styles he found in the language and suggested that 'the change from one to the other is often sudden and arbitrary. Each element has to be accepted for what it is, and yet a harmony must be found between them' (Programme Note to *Love's Labour's Lost*, 1965). Finding that harmony took time, and perhaps Barton was lucky that thirteen years elapsed between his two productions; Guthrie had only four years between his productions and seems not to have done much re-thinking, while Brook's 1947 production was essentially the same as the one he had directed in 1946. In the intervening years, Barton had directed many more of Shakespeare's plays. He had also married Anne Righter in 1968, and the connection between her writing about Shakespeare and his productions of the plays is one that seems evident. Yet, as Michael L. Greenwald points out in discussing Barton's famous 1969 production of *Twelfth Night*, 'whether Mr. Barton's ideas grew from Mrs. Barton's emerging criticism or vice-versa cannot be accurately determined' (Greenwald, p. 87). But it seems more than coincidental that the influential reading of *Love's Labour's Lost*, developed in 1953 by Anne Barton, alluded to in a study of Shakespeare's theatrical self-consciousness (Righter, 1962) and revised into the introduction to the play in the *Riverside Shakespeare* (1974), is very much the reading that the 1978 production would embody so fully: the sense of two worlds, the emphasis on the importance of keeping oaths, the necessity of growing up. Anne Barton's *Riverside Shakespeare* introduction appeared, in condensed form, as the programme note for the 1978 production, and her description of the play's conclusion draws together the complex stage action of the Pageant of the Nine Worthies and the reaction of the young men to the performance: 'Gently but firmly, the men are sent away to learn something that the women have known all along: how to accommodate speech to facts and to emotional realities, as opposed to using it as a means of evasion, idle amusement, or unthinking cruelty.' Just as Anne Barton began her 1953 essay on *Love's Labour's Lost* by talking not about the play's beginning but about its end, so John Barton began in 1978 by asking us to look at fallen leaves; just as Anne Barton ended her essay by speaking of 'the concrete reality of the world into which the characters are about to journey' (p. 425), John Barton reminded his audiences, onstage and offstage, of the 'staring owl', present not just in the imitations of the actors but in the offstage cry of a 'real' owl. Staging *Love's Labour's Lost* as a play with serious ideas, or even serious moments, began in the theatre with the work of Guthrie, Brook and Hunt; Anne Barton's 1953 essay established that seriousness for the academic world; John Barton's 1978 production represents the culmination of years of theatrical and academic investigation of the play's inner life, the meaning beneath its brilliant linguistic surface.

Suggesting the feelings beneath the words – finding what Stanislavsky called the 'subtext' – was one of the great achievements of Barton's 1978 production and prompts some speculation about production choices for *Love's Labour's Lost* since 1978, and production choices in the future. In the same year that Barton produced the play with a subtlety and melancholy that evoked comparisons with Chekhov for many reviewers (although the characters wore vaguely Elizabethan dress), Robin Phillips in Stratford, Ontario, moved the play into the early twentieth century, just before 1914; in so doing Phillips seemed to work from a concept of society that we also associate with Chekhov's plays. Reviewing that production, and the choice of period, Ralph Berry called the nineteenth century (which he defines as approximately 1814–1912) 'the most vivid of all preceding centuries to us, and the most apt for exploitation' precisely because it is 'the great age of property' (*Shakespeare Quarterly*, p. 172), an age when 'people are distinguishable by dress, manner, accent, calling, and moreover compose a society highly conscious of the minutest distinctions' (p. 173). Such reliance on external signals is, for Berry, 'the texture of the actors' being. Ibsen and Chekhov are unthinkable without it' – and he argues that 'Renaissance dress muffles or mutes the truth of the forms' (p.173). Thus Berry's reference to Chekhov emphasises a richly defined (and often wealthy, or formerly wealthy) society. His choosing of 1914 as the 'end' of the nineteenth century stresses the importance of the First World War as the demise of the polite formalities – in dress, manners, politics, and war – of the previous centuries. Like the people in Madame Ranevskaya's household, the courtiers in *Love's Labour's Lost* participate in their failure through their immature (and to some, even callous) behaviour. Phillips, according to Berry, seems to have kept the pageant and the courtiers' comments relatively good-humoured, but shattered the calm exit:

> Navarre spoke the last words, which stayed at 'The words of Mercury are harsh after the songs of Apollo,' and he turned to lead his guests out of the park. The front stage, containing the courtiers, was darkened; the rear stage, with spectators peering in through the park railings, luridly lit up. A distant rumbling was heard, over the horizon. The principals paused, looking at each other, puzzled. Was it thunder? Or gunfire? The belle époque ended with the guns of the Marne on the horizon, as in the text Fame yields to Death. This was an ending with hints of Brook's *Marat/Sade* and Chekhov, pure theatre, and as imaginative as correct. (p. 174)

Such an ending also evokes Shaw's *Heartbreak House*, his 'fantasia in the Russian manner'. In that play, as the preface makes clear, Shaw equates his careless people with 'cultured, leisured Europe before the war' (p.7) and points out that he withheld the play from production until 1919 'for the Germans might on any night have turned the last act from play into earnest' (p. 48), with real bombs instead of stage explosions. The preface gives Shaw's play a particular historical dimension, as does Phillips' extra-textual ending; Phillips thus raises the question of what shatters *Love's Labour's Lost*'s gracious world, at least for the moment. Is it an unstoppable historical force – whether the First World War, or the coming of Marcade to announce the death of the King of France – or have these young men created the problems themselves, and thus unleashed those forces of history? As I read Barton's 1978 production, the problem was essentially internal, created by the immaturity of the young men; their own 'pageant' of Muscovites, as well as their treatment of the Worthies, shows that they need to go away and think before they are ready to marry the women. Phillips's production offers a slightly more political view, if only because he set the play in an era which is closer to our time and made the young men soldiers; 'Navarre and his followers made their entry as young cavalry officers straight from exercising their horses, smoking, nonchalant' (p. 173). Berry's description implies that on one level these men were merely *playing* at being soldiers, and thus one might well associate them with the 'careless, leisured' people of whom Shaw spoke. The question of whether the destruction comes from within or without has no single answer, but it suggests possibilities for settings of *Love's Labour's Lost* which will continue to raise such problems.

Both of these productions focus, to a large extent, on the immaturity of the young men, and that focus has continued in two subsequent productions at Stratford-upon-Avon, one in 1984, directed by Barry Kyle and one in 1990, directed by Terry Hands. But the corollary of this choice in these later productions was that the men were too young to be of any real interest to the women. Little sexual chemistry existed between the men and the women – a problem which likewise plagued the BBC production of 1984. Kenneth Branagh's boyish Navarre (Stratford-upon-Avon, 1984) had an eager puppy-dog quality as well as a slight stutter which appeared at moments of panic. Branagh's king was a nice fellow, but not very bright, falling into Costard's mispronunciation of 'virgin' as 'wirgin' and arguing 'for it was proclaimed wirgin' and then angrily correcting himself. When reading the letter from the King of France, he tried desperately to sound like an assured lawyer and ended up stumbling over words, putting in extra syllables of indecision and constantly having to refer back to the letter. His denseness is, in part, inherent in the text, but Branagh added yet another level when he first hid behind a small potted plant in IV.iii and then erupted to confront Longaville and Dumaine, yelling at them 'I have been closely shrouded in this bush' before suddenly realising that he was still carrying the bush around with him. The lack of hiding places on Bob Crowley's elegant and fragile-looking set meant that in the same scene Berowne (Roger Rees) had to position himself behind a headless statue of Cupid, and could not, of course, resist the temptation to pose *en attitude*. As in the 1968 Stratford, Connecticut production, where the young men hid behind potted plants rather than real trees, immaturity turned to physical silliness.

Casting Simon Russell Beale as Navarre (Stratford-upon-Avon, 1990) was, like casting Richard Griffiths, a somewhat curious choice, since Beale has made his reputation primarily in comic roles, including an entire season of Restoration fops in the Swan; he did, however, play another king during the 1990 season, Marlowe's Edward II. Short, slightly plump, blond, he seemed an entirely non-threatening figure; when he read Armado's greeting to him as 'sole dominator of Navarre', the other men laughed until he quelled them with a look. This was a king whose pen ran out of ink half-way through his signing of the oath and who, running in for the hunt before IV.i, managed to fall down the gentle rise at the back of the stage. When he could not immediately come up with an answer to Berowne's question in I.i, 'What is the end of study, let me know?' (I.i.55), he looked over to Longaville and then to

Dumaine, hoping that they might help him out, though he did finally manage a response. And when he met the Princess, he struggled between 1) anger at her father's letter, 2) embarrassment at his own anger (one can see him thinking to himself that perhaps calling Aquitaine 'gelded' was a bit extreme), and 3) awe at her beauty.

Both Branagh's and Beale's readings contained echoes of Richard Griffiths's likeable King. But instead of balancing the King's obvious uncertainty and naiveté with someone who also has those qualities, both the 1984 and the 1990 productions cast as the Princess actresses of cool composure. Emily Richard (1984) has a strikingly deep voice which added to the sense of self-control as well as control of any social situation; she was, in Russell Jackson's description, 'older than Navarre and much more mature in her emotions' (p. 90). Jackson contrasts this relationship with that of Griffiths and Du Sautoy, pointing out, 'In Barton's production, the Princess's self-confidence and maturity were in as critical a stage of development as Navarre's; in Kyle's the relationship is more like Treplev and Arkadina' (p. 90). A similarly motherly tone pervaded the BBC's production, since Maureen Lipman seemed noticeably older as well as more mature than Jonathan Kent's Navarre.

Carol Royle, who played the Princess in 1990, was also cool and assured, wearing a gorgeous mauve dress with a huge hoop skirt, the bodice of the dress trimmed with military-looking stripes. Her parasol and her hoop always created space around her, making her virtually untouchable. In the hunting scene (IV.i), her costume was less formal, with a low-cut blouse, but she also wore a leopard skin wrapped around her skirt and a small tiara, topped with a crescent moon, the emblem of the chaste huntress/goddess Diana. Indeed, in her blonde prettiness and stunning clothes, she evoked the present-day Diana, Princess of Wales. But more important than her clothes was the tone of play-acting which pervaded her performance. She seemed surprised, but in an affected way, when she responded to Boyet's 'Navarre is infected' with a wide-eyed 'With what?' Was she really surprised, or just pretending to be, or was the pretence a cover-up? In IV.i Royle's Princess spoke with a sense of feigned hurt on 'short-liv'd pride! Not fair? alack for woe!' (IV.i.15) in response to the Forester's stumbling remarks. Only at the end did she seem both composed and gentle in her treatment of the King, but since the composure had always been present, there was no noticeable change when she heard about her father's death.

Indeed, her white off-the-shoulder gown and the moon-topped tiara made her look like a queen already.

The casting choices for the Princess in the 1984 and 1990 Stratford-upon-Avon productions and the 1984 BBC production could spring from several sources. Interestingly, they do *not* reflect the influence of a repertory company, since for both Emily Richard and Carol Royle, the Princess was the only role each actress played in that particular Stratford season. While Moshinsky did use some actors who had previously worked with him or in other BBC Shakespeare productions, his casting of Maureen Lipman went far outside the usual group. One might argue that since the women in the play clearly triumph over the men, it makes sense to have their leader be a strong, even dominant woman. Or perhaps, like Moshinsky, both Kyle and Hands chose to underscore the sense in which the love is primarily an illusion at which we smile. If so, then the ending is less surprising and less painful than if the audience has been asked to believe, even fleetingly, in the reciprocal feelings of the men and women.

In all of these productions – Kyle, Moshinsky, Hands – the disparity between the emotional and social maturity of the Princess and that of the King makes it difficult to believe that the Princess ever feels, or could feel, anything for him. A schoolboy crush on an older and more sophisticated woman is plausible, but not a reciprocal feeling. The problem of whether the audience believes that the men and women really do love each other is, as I have suggested in the opening chapter, one that is inherent in the play. Indeed, it is a question which comes up in a number of Shakespeare's comedies. Women such as Julia, Portia, Rosalind and Viola seem so much more aware of themselves and of the complexities of their lives than do the men they end up with, Proteus, Bassanio, Orlando and Orsino, that literary and theatrical audiences continue to question the happiness of the plays' 'ever after'. Barton's solution – showing both men and women as insecure to some extent – allows the audience to see the possibility of reciprocal love developing even though we also understand that whatever these people feel for each other needs time for testing and for growth. Later productions have been less successful in conveying such a possibility.

While casting choices for the King and the Princess can balance, or unbalance, the potential for love between them, the relationship between Berowne and Rosaline always oscillates between the wit which both characters possess and the extent to which love and/or sexual attraction will reveal itself in spite of the defence of wit. In 1984 and (although to a lesser extent) in 1990, Rosaline's tendency towards cool detachment, both within the group of women and in relation to Berowne, made it more difficult to see her interest in him. The identification of the addressee of Armado's letter offers a useful moment for comparison. In Shakespeare's text Costard announces 'I have a letter from Monsieur Berowne to one Lady Rosaline' (IV.i. 53-4), and then a few lines later, Boyet, letter in hand, announces: 'This letter is mistook; it importeth none here: / It is writ to Jaquenetta' (IV.i.58-9). In Barton's 1978 production, Boyet's line about the letter being for Jaquenetta does not come until he is deep into reading the letter. The phrase 'the pernicious and indubitate beggar Zenelophon' so puzzles him that he turns over the letter and sees that it was meant for Jaquenetta. Rosaline tries to get the letter as soon as she hears it is for her, smiles with the opening lines, and then begins to share Boyet's bewilderment – how *could* Berowne write such stuff? Once she knows that the letter is not for her, she joins the other women and participates with pleasure in the question-and-answer game. In 1984, Josette Simon is isolated from the women when Boyet discovers that the letter is for Jaquenetta (the line remains where it is in the text), so she simply doesn't hear that there's a mistake. But she also doesn't join in the game, and the fact that the other women know what is going on when she does not creates a sense of coolness within the group. Terry Hands, in 1990, also keeps the line where it occurs in the text, but Amanda Root's Rosaline hears the line, leaps to the conclusion that Berowne is writing to someone else, and is at first a bit hurt. As she listens she becomes increasingly perplexed by this letter; although she's angry when she hears at the end that the letter is from Armado, we can see that she is also relieved.

The reaction during the letter scene is crucial for Amanda Root if we are to believe her last moments with Berowne (Ralph Fiennes). He stretches his hand out to Rosaline, 'Studies my lady?', and moves down centre, then kneels, facing upstage. She stands above him, watching his reaction; when she says 'You shall this twelvemonth term from day to day / Visit the speechless sick', he rises slightly as if about to protest and then sinks back to his knees. On her speech of explanation, she takes his hands and bends down to kiss him; as she does, he rises and holds her for a moment, then says, almost cheerfully, 'I'll jest a twelvemonth in an hospital.' But in 1984, Josette Simon's Rosaline only touches Berowne's cheek, in the one tender moment they have together; Roger Rees's Berowne does not try to touch her, but simply puts his hand to his cheek after she moves away, touching the place she has touched.

Given the separation of the men and women at the end, one can reasonably argue for a variety of characterisations: silly men involved in a silly oath (one thinks of the solemn procession at the beginning of the 1973 production when the men ceremoniously strip off their cloaks, hats, gloves and jackets and throw them into a waiting coffin); immature men swearing a naively conceived oath; sophisticated women who hide their true feelings; sceptical women; and so on. Similarly, one can imagine varying degrees of affected behaviour with Armado and the rustics, although the tendency in this century (with the exception of the Michael Kahn production) has been to invest at least Armado, and often Holofernes and Nathaniel, with some dignity. The connection of Armado with Don Quixote has occurred to a number of actors and directors. Paul Rogers, who began as Dull in Hugh Hunt's 1949 production, but who then took over as Armado, writes:

> Studying Armado, the fantastic Spaniard, it seems almost impossible that the other great Don has had no part of Armado's making. Armado's view of love is very 'de la Mancha.' At the time of writing, the Spaniard, like the Jew in *The Merchant of Venice*, was good for a laugh and a hearty boo; but on each occasion the character ran away with his creator. The stage is set for Armado to be merely a figure of fun, but his goodness and simple honour take hold of our affections and in the end he is wringing our hearts with as simple a line as 'I have no shirt.' One laughs, but underneath is an awareness of something deep, brave, noble and tragicomical. We are well aware that the child bragging in Jaquenetta's belly is certainly Costard's. The Don is more fortunate: most readily and nobly he embraces paternity. (Rogers, Introduction to *Love's Labour's Lost*, p.10).

Such interpretations lead naturally to the complexities of the final scene, since if the rustics are only silly, then the nobles' comments on the Pageant seem appropriate. But when the audience perceives not just the affectations of Armado and Holofernes, but also their sincere goodwill and efforts to recreate an heroic past, the interrupting commentary sounds callous and bullying. And the more a director turns to an autumnal reading of the play, the more often Armado becomes the focus of the ending. In 1949, 'the bemused touchstone of the play is left alone (or, as Hugh Hunt envisaged it, with a sheltering arm about his lady's shoulders) to bid you all the gentlest of good nights' (Rogers, p. 10). Even when Boyet spoke the final lines in Barton's 1965 production, Armado knelt centre stage. In 1984, he held Jaquenetta's hand as they left, while in 1990, they were seen embracing far upstage. A poignant version at the Guthrie in 1974 showed 'Don Adriano and the pregnant Jaquenetta. The old gentleman beckoned to her, kissed her hand, saluted, and bowed as she toddled away; then, as autumn leaves fell, he wrapped himself in his cape, lifted tearful eyes, and made his exit' (Priscilla Shaw, p. 347).

As soon as one starts thinking about Armado, questions arise about Jaquenetta and her behaviour; the more sexually forthcoming she is, the more foolish he may look, loving a 'light wench', vowing to 'hold the plough three years' for a woman who may be pregnant with his child but is equally likely to be carrying Costard's baby. Thus, in the RSC's 1973 production, Costard and Jaquenetta used the reading of Berowne's sonnet (IV.ii) as a time for increasingly passionate stroking, interrupted only by looks from Holofernes, while in 1984 Holofernes and Nathaniel, with Jaquenetta sitting between them, were both trying to attract her attention, while her wide-eyed rapture showed clearly how thrilled she was to think that anyone might address such words to her. In 1990, Jaquenetta's sexual overtures were both friendly and forthright. Her kiss to Nathaniel after he had read the sonnet to her reduced the curate to jelly, while in IV.iii, when Berowne fell to his knees, confessing 'Guilty, my lord, guilty!', she took that as an invitation and began hugging him and even starting to undress him. In one sense, Armado looks silly in his infatuation with any of these Jaquenettas, but he also gains a kind of dignity, especially when he insists that he will stay with her.

Yet another kind of relationship which can vary greatly in performance is that of Boyet to the women. Casting choices may define the character, as can be seen in the contrast between a particularly experienced actor (Brewster Mason in 1965) and a younger and less experienced actor (Alan Rickman in 1978). J. W. Lambert headed his review of the 1965 production 'Oh Boyet!' (*The Sunday Times*, 11 April 1965) and noted that Boyet became 'the dominant character' to whom the Princess turned 'for guidance in matters of policy' and whose 'automatic authority' the young men recognised. Mason's authority thus set the tone for the courts of Navarre and France – *everyone* looked younger next to him. In 1978, the choice of a much younger actor led to moments where Boyet seemed to be trying to establish his authority, such as in his longish speech in II.i when he says he will go to look for the King but doesn't actually leave. During the Pageant of the Nine Worthies, Rickman's Boyet seemed just as much of a bully as Berowne, Dumaine and Longaville, joining in the sarcastic commentary with evident relish. In a way, this younger Boyet was lucky not to be serving a Princess as experienced as Emily Richard or Carol Royle; they would, one feels, have had little patience with him. It's difficult to know if the choice of the younger actor was, for Barton, simply a function of the repertory situation or not. Given his emphasis in 1978 on the social awkwardness of both the King and the Princess, one can imagine that a strong and dominating Boyet, such as the one Brewster Mason gave Barton in 1965, might have been most appropriate. But the absence of such authority made even more noticeable the Princess's struggle to maintain control of the diplomatic situation, even when she was clearly unused to such efforts and was, at the same time, falling in love with the King.

Though *Love's Labour's Lost* lacks the usual happy ending of Shakespeare's comedies, the story of its life on stage, from the middle of the nineteenth century to the present day, certainly reads as one of discovery and triumph. To go from 200 years of neglect to regular, and regularly successful productions is noteworthy. The interplay between stage production and critical re-evaluation testifies to the stage's ability to bring about, as with John Dover Wilson, a 'conversion' to the play's real power. Or one thinks of Paul Rogers beginning his introduction to The Folio Society's text of the play with the confession, 'Shamelessly, I admit I am in love with *Love's Labour's Lost.*' He goes on to attribute that love to experience: 'The condition is shared, I will hazard a guess, by most players fortunate enough to have performed it at any time, and certainly by all of us who were in Hugh Hunt's enchanted production at the New Theatre – the Old Vic production of 1949' (Rogers, p. 7).

My own experience with the play, directing it at The University of Iowa in 1982, with a cast made up almost entirely of undergraduates, combines a number of the reactions to the play that critics and actors have had: fear, anxiety, excitement, and, finally, delight. At the opening round of the auditions, I did not even ask students to read from the text, because I was afraid that they might be so put off by the difficulty of the language that they would not want to be in the play. When we first read the play together, there were long stretches of stumbling over lines as well as many questions about obscure words and Latin phrases. But there was also, even at the first reading, one wonderful period of relaxation and laughter when we got to IV.iii, the overhearing scene. The joke is so beautifully constructed that the students found themselves listening and enjoying the many reversals of the scene. During rehearsals, I found the young men and women who played the four pairs of lovers often sitting on opposite sides of the room, without any prompting from me. The 'battle of the sexes' flared not just with the lines of the play but in comments made by the actors; the women found the men's behaviour silly, while the men wondered why the women were playing 'hard to get'. The distinction between groups of characters in the play revealed itself naturally as we worked on various scenes. Not until the final scene, and even then, only in the latter half of that long scene, does Shakespeare bring together all of his characters. For most of the play, and for more of the rehearsal period, Armado and Moth formed a group, as did Holofernes, Nathaniel and Dull. Indeed, the rehearsals for the Pageant of the Nine Worthies went on by themselves; after some preliminary discussion, I simply told the Worthies to go off and work on each 'act' and come back to show me what they had created. Thus each character got to define his own Worthy. In the case of Moth, a twelve-year-old girl, this led to radical restagings of the fight between the infant Hercules and the serpents, including one performance when, after a ferocious battle, Moth lost and lay prostrate under the stuffed animals!

Most interestingly, the reaction of the young actors moved from detachment to sympathy. At the end of the first read-through, we talked about the play and I asked what people thought about the way in which the young men treated the Worthies. Most were sure that these simple-minded characters deserved all the sarcasm heaped upon them. Then came a very slow and painstaking reading of the play again, extending over several sessions, with many stops for explanation and paraphrase. When we came to the moment when Berowne, Boyet and Dumaine jeer Holofernes/Judas Maccabeus off the stage, and Holofernes turns to them with 'This is not generous, not gentle, not humble', the room became very quiet. The actor playing Dumaine was horrified. 'We're such shits', he said. 'The audience is going to hate us – how will we ever be saved?'

BIBLIOGRAPHY

Allen, Shirley S., *Samuel Phelps and Sadler's Wells Theatre*, Middletown, CT, 1971.

Barber, C. L., *Shakespeare's Festive Comedy*, Princeton, NJ, 1959.

Barnet, Sylvan (ed.), *The Complete Signet Classic Shakespeare*, New York, 1963.

Barton, John, *Playing Shakespeare*, London, 1984.

Beauman, Sally, *The Royal Shakespeare Company: A History of Ten Decades*, Oxford, 1982.

Beckerman, Bernard, 'Stratford (Connecticut) Revisited', *Shakespeare Quarterly*, 19, 1968, 377-80.

Berry, Ralph 'The Words of Mercury', *Shakespeare Survey*, 22, 1969, 69-77.

——, 'Stratford Festival Canada', *Shakespeare Quarterly*, 31, 1980, 167-75.

——, *On Directing Shakespeare*, revised edition, London, 1989.

Brook, Peter, *The Empty Space*, London, 1972 (first published in 1968).

——, *The Shifting Point*, New York, 1987.

Brown, John Russell, 'The Royal Shakespeare Company 1965', *Shakespeare Survey*, 19, 1965, 111-18.

Buckley, William F., 'The Beatles and the Guru', quoted in *The Beatles Reader*, ed. Charles P. Neises, Ann Arbor, MI, 1984.

Byrne, M. St Clare, 'Fifty Years of Shakespearian Production, 1898-1948', *Shakespeare Survey*, 2, 1949, 1-20.

Carroll, William C., *The Great Feast of Language in 'Love's Labour's Lost'*, Princeton, NJ, 1976.

Cook, Ann Jennalie, *The Privileged Playgoers of Shakespeare's London, 1576-1642*, Princeton, NJ, 1981.

Cooper, Roberta Krensky, *The American Shakespeare Theatre: Stratford 1955-1985*, Washington, DC, 1986.

Crosse, Gordon, *Shakespearean Playgoing 1890-1952*, London, 1953.

David, Richard (ed.), *Love's Labour's Lost*, The Arden Shakespeare, London, 1951.

——, 'Shakespeare's Comedies and the Modern Stage', *Shakespeare Survey*, 4, 1951, 129-35.

——, *Shakespeare in the Theatre*, Cambridge, 1978.

Dickens, Charles, *Charles Dickens' Uncollected Writings from 'Household Words' 1850-1859*, ed. Harry Stone, Bloomington, IN, and London, 1968.

Ellis, Herbert A., *Shakespeare's Lusty Punning in 'Love's Labour's Lost'*, The Hague, 1973.

Fenwick, Henry, 'The Production', in *Love's Labour's Lost*, BBC edition, London, 1986, pp. 17-25.

Foss, George R., *What the Author Meant*, London, 1932.

Goddard, Harold C., *The Meaning of Shakespeare*, Chicago, IL, 1951.

Granville-Barker, Harley, *Prefaces to Shakespeare*, First Series, London, 1927.

Greenwald, Michael L., *Directions by Indirections: John Barton of the Royal Shakespeare Company*, Newark, DE, 1985.

Guthrie, Tyrone, *A Life in the Theatre*, New York, 1959.

Habicht, Werner, 'Tree Properties and Tree Scenes in Elizabethan Theater', *Renaissance Drama*, n.s. 4, 1971, 69-92.

Hallinan, Tim, 'Jonathan Miller on The Shakespeare Plays', *Shakespeare Quarterly*, 32, 1981, 134-45.

Harbage, Alfred, '*Love's Labor's Lost* and the Early Shakespeare', *Philological Quarterly*, 41, 1962, 18-36.

Hayman, Ronald, *Playback*, London, 1973.

Henslowe, Philip, *Henslowe's Diary*, ed. R. A. Foakes and R. T. Rickert, Cambridge, 1961.

Hibbard, G. R. (ed.), *Love's Labour's Lost*, The Oxford Shakespeare, Oxford, 1990.

Hodgdon, Barbara, 'Rehearsal Process as Critical Practice: John Barton's 1978 *Love's Labour's Lost*', *Theatre History Studies*, 8, 1988. I have also consulted Hodgdon's unpublished notes on Barton's rehearsals.

Hogan, Charles Beecher, *Shakespeare in the Theatre 1701-1800*, Oxford, 1952.

Holding, Edith Margaret Mary, '*Love's Labour's Lost* and the English Stage, 1762-1949', Dissertation, The Shakespeare Institute, 1978.

Hunt, Hugh, *Old Vic Prefaces*, London, 1954.

Jackson, Barry, 'Producing the Comedies', *Shakespeare Survey*, 8, 1955, 74-80.

Jackson, Russell, 'Love's Labour's Lost', *Cahiers élisabéthains*, 28, 1985, 89-92.

Johnson, Samuel, *Selections from Johnson on Shakespeare*, ed. Bertrand H. Bronson with Jean M. O'Meara, New Haven, CT and London, 1986.

Jones, Gordon P., 'Nahum Tate is Alive and Well: Elijah Moshinsky's BBC Shakespeare Productions', in *Shakespeare on Television*, ed. J. C. Bulman and H. R. Coursen, Hanover, NH, 1988, pp. 192-200.

Kahn, Michael, interview with Miriam Gilbert, May 1989.

Kerrigan, John (ed.), *Love's Labour's Lost*, New Penguin Shakespeare, London, 1982.

Lamb, Mary Ellen, 'The Nature of Topicality in "Love's Labour's Lost"', *Shakespeare Survey*, 38, 1985, 49-59.

Levenson, Jill, *Shakespeare in Performance: Romeo and Juliet*, Manchester, 1987.

Levey, Michael, *Rococo to Revolution: Major Trends in Eighteenth-Century*

Painting, London, 1966.

Monck, Nugent, 'The Maddermarket Theatre and the Playing of Shakespeare', *Shakespeare Survey*, 12, 1959, 71-5.

Morley, Henry, *The Journal of a London Playgoer, from 1851 to 1866*, London, 1891.

Mulryne, J. R., 'The Owl and the Cuckoo: Shakespeare's Natural Dialogue', in *Le Dialogue au temps de la Renaissance*, ed. M. T. Jones-Davies, Paris, 1984.

Phelps, W. May and John Forbes-Robertson, *The Life and Life-Work of Samuel Phelps*, London, 1886.

Powell, Jocelyn, 'John Lyly and the Language of Play', in *Elizabethan Theatre*, ed. John Russell Brown and Bernard Harris, London, 1966.

Reynolds, G. F., '"Trees" on the Stage of Shakespeare', *Modern Philology*, 5, 1907, 153-68.

Rhodes, Ernest L., *Henslowe's Rose: The Stage and Staging*, Lexington, KY, 1976.

Righter, Anne (Anne Barton), *Shakespeare and the Idea of the Play*, London, 1962.

Roesen, Bobbyann (Anne Barton), '*Love's Labour's Lost*', *Shakespeare Quarterly*, 4, 1953, 411-26.

Rogers, Paul, Introduction to *Love's Labour's Lost*, London, 1959.

Saccio, Peter, *The Court Comedies of John Lyly: A Study in Allegorical Dramaturgy*, Princeton, NJ, 1969.

Shaw, George Bernard, *Heartbreak House*, Penguin edition, London, 1964.

——, *Shaw on Shakespeare*, ed. Edwin Wilson, London, 1961.

Shaw, Priscilla D., in *Shakespeare Around the Globe: A Guide to Notable Postwar Revivals*, ed. Samuel L. Leiter, New York, 1986, pp. 346-7.

Smith, Peter D., 'The 1969 Season at Stratford, Connecticut', *Shakespeare Quarterly*, 20, 1969, 447-50.

Speaight, Robert, *The Property Basket: Recollections of a Divided Life*, London, 1970.

Stanislavsky, Constantin, *Creating a Role*, trans. Elizabeth Reynolds Hapgood, New York, 1961.

Stone, George Winchester, 'Garrick and an unknown operatic version of *Love's Labour's Lost*', *Review of English Studies*, 15, 1939, 323-8.

Strutt, Joseph, *The Sports and Pastimes of the People of England*, ed. William Hone, London, 1898 (first published 1801).

The Students, London, 1969, facsimile of 1762 edition.

Taylor, Gary, *Reinventing Shakespeare*, London, 1989.

Teague, Frances, 'The Shakespeare Plays on TV', *Shakespeare on Film Newsletter*, 9:1, December 1986, reprinted in *Shakespeare on Television*, ed. J. C. Bulman and H. R. Coursen, Hanover, NH, 1988, pp.312-13.

Traversi, D. A., *An Approach to Shakespeare*, 3rd edition, London, 1968.

Trewin, J. C., *The Birmingham Repertory Theatre, 1913-1963*, London, 1963.

——, *Peter Brook: A Biography*, London, 1971.

Tricomi, Albert H., 'The Witty Idealization of the French Court in *Love's Labor's Lost*', *Shakespeare Studies*, 12, 1979, 25-33.

Van Doren, Mark, *Shakespeare*, London, 1941.

Waller, Gary F., 'Decentering the Bard: The BBC-TV Shakespeare and Some Implications for Criticism and Teaching', in *Shakespeare on Television*, ed. J. C. Bulman and H. R. Coursen, Hanover, NH, 1988, pp. 18-30.

Warren, Roger, 'A Year of Comedies: Stratford 1978', *Shakespeare Survey*, 32, 1979, 201-9.

Wiles, David, *Shakespeare's Clown: Actor and text in the Elizabethan playhouse*, Cambridge, 1987.

Williams, Clifford John, *Madame Vestris: A Theatrical Biography*, London, 1973.

Williamson, Audrey, *Old Vic Drama*, London, 1948.

Willis, Susan, *The BBC Shakespeare Plays: Making the Televised Canon*, Chapel Hill, NC, 1991.

Wilson, John Dover, *Shakespeare's Happy Comedies*, London, 1962.

APPENDIX

A. Some significant twentieth-century productions of *Love's Labour's Lost*

1918	George Foss	London
1919	Barry Jackson	Birmingham (revived 1925)
1932	Tyrone Guthrie	London
1936	Tyrone Guthrie	London
1946	Peter Brook	Stratford-upon-Avon (revived 1947)
1948	Hugh Hunt	London
1956	Peter Hall	Stratford-upon-Avon
1965	John Barton	Stratford-upon-Avon
1968	Michael Kahn	Stratford, Connecticut
1968	Laurence Olivier	London
1973	David Jones	Stratford-upon-Avon
1974	Michael Langham	Minneapolis
1978	John Barton	Stratford-upon-Avon
1978	Robin Phillips	Stratford, Ontario
1984	Barry Kyle	Stratford-upon-Avon
1984	Elijah Moshinsky	BBC television
1990	Terry Hands	Stratford-upon-Avon

B. Major actors and staff for productions discussed in this volume

Sadler's Wells Theatre, 30 September 1857
Director: Samuel Phelps Designer: C. S. James

King	Frederick Robinson	Moth	Rose Williams
Berowne	Henry Marston	Costard	Lewis Ball
Princess	Mrs Charles Young	Holofernes	W. 'Pepper' Williams
Rosaline	Helen Fitzpatrick	Nathaniel	C. Fenton
Boyet	J. W. Ray	Dull	Mr Meagreson
Armado	Samuel Phelps		

Old Vic Theatre, 14 September 1936
Director: Tyrone Guthrie Designer: Molly MacArthur

King	Michael Redgrave	*Armado*	Ernest Milton
Berowne	Alec Clunes	*Moth*	Gordon Miller
Princess	Rachel Kempson	*Costard*	Frederick Bennett
Rosaline	Margaretta Scott	*Holofernes*	Evan John
Boyet	Alec Guinness	*Nathaniel*	John Abbott

Royal Shakespeare Theatre, 26 April 1946
Director: Peter Brook Designer: Reginald Leefe Music: Allan Gray

King	Paul Stephenson	*Moth*	David O'Brien
Berowne	David King-Wood	*Costard*	Robert Vernon
Princess	Valerie Taylor	*Holofernes*	Hugh Griffith
Rosaline	Ruth Lodge	*Nathaniel*	Dudley Jones
Boyet	Julian Somers	*Dull*	Vernon Fortescue
Armado	Paul Scofield		

New Theatre, 11 October 1949
Director: Hugh Hunt Designer: Berkeley Sutcliffe Music: Herbert Menges

King	Michael Aldridge	*Armado*	Baliol Holloway
Berowne	Michael Redgrave		(later, Paul Rogers)
Princess	Angela Baddeley	*Costard*	George Benson
Rosaline	Diana Churchill	*Holofernes*	Mark Dignam
Boyet	Walter Hudd	*Nathaniel*	Miles Malleson
Moth	Brian Smith	*Dull*	Paul Rogers

Royal Shakespeare Theatre, Stratford-upon-Avon, 7 April 1965
Director: John Barton Designer: Sally Jacobs Music: Guy Woolfenden

King	Charles Kay	*Moth*	Philip Meredith
Berowne	Charles Thomas	*Costard*	Tim Wylton
Princess	Glenda Jackson	*Holofernes*	Tony Church
Rosaline	Janet Suzman	*Nathaniel*	Timothy West
Boyet	Brewster Mason	*Dull*	David Waller
Armado	William Squire		

American Shakespeare Festival, Stratford, Connecticut, 23 June 1968
Director: Michael Kahn Set Designer: Will Steven Armstrong
Costume Designer: Jane Greenwood Music: Frangipane & Dante

King	Charles Siebert	*Moth*	Bryan Young
Berowne	Lawrence Pressman	*Costard*	William Hickey
Princess	Diana van der Vlis	*Holofernes*	Stefan Gierasch
Rosaline	Denise Huot	*Nathaniel*	Ken Parker
Boyet	Thomas Ruisinger	*Dull*	Rex Everhart
Armado	Josef Sommer		

Royal Shakespeare Theatre, Stratford-upon-Avon, 7 August 1973
Director: David Jones Designers: Timothy O'Brien and Tazeena Firth
Music: William Southgate

King	Bernard Lloyd	*Moth*	Tony Valls/
Berowne	Ian Richardson		Joseph Murru
Princess	Susan Fleetwood	*Costard*	Timothy Dalton
Rosaline	Estelle Kohler	*Holofernes*	Derek Smith
Boyet	Sebastian Shaw	*Nathaniel*	Jeffrey Dench
Armado	Tony Church	*Dull*	Denis Holmes

Royal Shakespeare Theatre, Stratford-upon-Avon, 11 August 1978
Director: John Barton Designer: Ralph Koltai Music: James Walker

King	Richard Griffiths	*Moth*	Jo James
Berowne	Michael Pennington	*Costard*	Allan Hendrick
Princess	Carmen Du Sautoy	*Holofernes*	Paul Brooke
Rosaline	Jane Lapotaire	*Nathaniel*	David Suchet
Boyet	Alan Rickman	*Dull*	David Lyon
Armado	Michael Hordern		

The BBC TV Shakespeare, first broadcast January 1985 (UK),
May 1985 (USA)
Director: Elijah Moshinsky Designer: Barbara Gosnold
Music:Stephen Oliver

King	Jonathan Kent	*Moth*	John Kane
Berowne	Mike Gwilym	*Costard*	Paul Jesson
Princess	Maureen Lipman	*Holofernes*	John Wells
Rosaline	Jenny Agutter	*Nathaniel*	John Burgess
Boyet	Clifford Rose	*Dull*	Frank Williams
Armado	David Warner		

Royal Shakespeare Theatre, Stratford-upon-Avon, 10 October 1984
Director: Barry Kyle Designer: Bob Crowley Music: Guy Woolfenden

King	Kenneth Branagh	*Armado*	Edward Petherbridge
Berowne	Roger Rees		(later Richard Easton)
Princess	Emily Richard	*Costard*	Brian Parr
Rosaline	Josette Simon	*Holofernes*	Christopher Benjamin
Boyet	John Carlisle	*Nathaniel*	John Rogan
Moth	Amanda Root	*Dull*	George Raistrick

Royal Shakespeare Theatre, Stratford-upon-Avon, 5 September 1990
Director: Terry Hands Designer: Timothy O'Brien
Music: Guy Woolfenden

King	Simon Russell Beale	*Moth*	Nicholas Besley/
Berowne	Ralph Fiennes		Jon-Sel Gourkan
Princess	Carol Royle	*Costard*	Lloyd Hutchinson
Rosaline	Amanda Root	*Holofernes*	David Troughton
Boyet	David Killick	*Nathaniel*	Paul Webster
Armado	John Wood	*Dull*	Richard Ridings

INDEX

Hodgdon, Barbara, 93, 98-9, 102, 106, 114
Hogan, Charles Beecher, 21-2
Holding, Edith Margaret Mary, 35
Holland, Mary, 112
Hordern, Michael, 106
Hunt, Hugh, 51-3, 55, 117, 123, 125

Isham, Gyles, 38

Jackson, Barry, 37, 41-3, 55
Jackson, Glenda, 94, 97
Jackson, Russell, 120
Jacobs, Sally, 94, 109-10
James, Jo, 59, 106
Johnson, Samuel, 1, 15, 26
Jones, David, 65, 73, 109, 115
Jones, Gordon P., 57-8, 60, 72, 75
Jonson, Ben, 8

Kahn, Michael, 78-91, 123
Kane, John, 58-9
Kay, Charles, 98
Kemp, Peter, 74
Kemp, Will, 16
Kempson, Rachel, 40
Kent, Jonathan, 120
Kerrigan, John, 1, 7-8
Koltai, Ralph, 97, 109-10
Kyd, Thomas 8
Kyle, Barry, 53, 109, 119, 121

Lamb, Mary Ellen, 6, 17-18
Lambert, J. W., 124
Lapotaire, Jane, 102
Lebor, Stanley, 95
Leefe, Reginald, 45
Levenson, Jill, 26
Levey, Michael, 49
Lipman, Maureen, 66-8, 97, 120-1
Lyly, John, 13-14

MacArthur, Molly, 39, 44
Macready, William Charles, 27
Maharishi Mahesh Yogi, 78, 90
Marlowe, Christopher, 17, 95, 119
Marston, John, 7
Mason, Brewster, 95, 124-5
Mathews, Charles John, 27

Messina, Cedric, 56-7
Miller, Gordon, 39-40, 59
Miller, Jonathan, 56-7, 75
Milton, Ernest, 40
Monck, Nugent, 38-9, 41
Morley, Henry, 32, 34-5
Moshinsky, Elijah, 56, 57-76, 77, 112, 121

Nashe, Thomas, 17, 77
Nunn, Trevor, 89, 93

O'Brien, David, 59
O'Brien, Timothy, 53
Olivier, Laurence, 40, 42
Oxenford, John, 32-5

painters and set/costume design
    Canaletto, 57
    Hals, Frans, 57
    Lancret, Nicolas, 45, 51, 54
    Manet, Édouard, 53-4
    Monet, Claude, 53-4
    Rembrandt, 57
    Rubens, Peter Paul, 57
    Titian, 57
    Velasquez, 48
    Vermeer, 57
    Veronese, 57
    Watteau, Jean-Antoine, 44-9, 51, 53-7, 64, 77
Papp, Joseph, 89
Pennington, Michael, 96-7, 104, 110
Peter, John, 92
Phelps, Samuel, 29-36, 37, 39, 42, 52
Phelps, W. May, 32-5
Phillips, Robin, 117-18
Planché, James Robinson, 27-9
Pope, Alexander, 26
Powell, Jocelyn, 14
Pressman, Lawrence, 88

Ralegh, Sir Walter, 32, 77
Redgrave, Michael, 40
Rees, Roger, 54, 119, 123
Reynolds, G. F., 8
Rhodes, Ernest L., 8
Richard, Emily, 120-1, 125